Fresh Ways with Poultry

BY

THE EDITORS OF TIME-LIFE BOOKS

TIME-LIFE BOOKS / ALEXANDRIA, VIRGINIA

Contents

Chicken with Peanuts and Ginger Sauce

Spicy Yogurt-Baked Chicken Thighs

Stir-Fried Chicken with Broccoli, Red Onions and Cashew Nuts

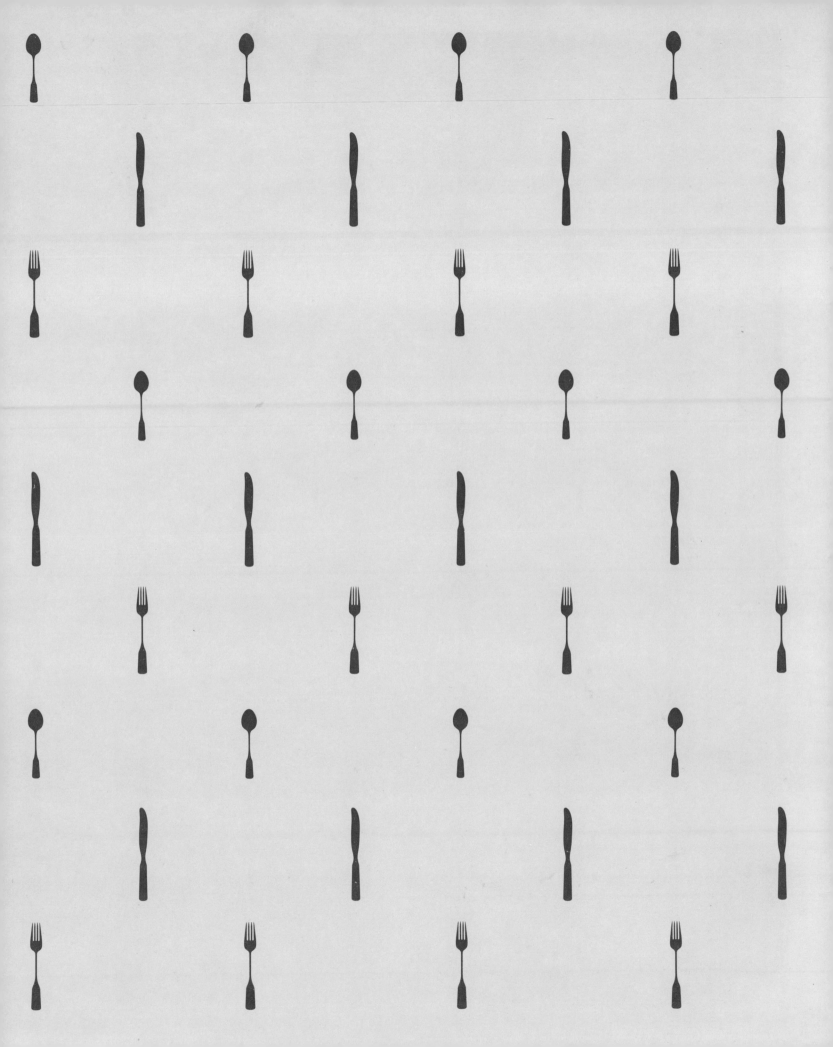

Fresh Ways with Poultry

Time-Life Books Inc.
is a wholly owned subsidiary of
TIME INCORPORATED

FOUNDER: Henry R. Luce 1898-1967

Editor-in-Chief: Henry Anatole Grunwald
President: J. Richard Munro
Chairman of the Board: Ralph P. Davidson
Corporate Editor: Ray Cave
Group Vice President, Books: Reginald K. Brack Jr.
Vice President, Books: George Artandi

TIME-LIFE BOOKS INC.

EDITOR: George Constable
Executive Editor: George Daniels
Editorial General Manager: Neal Goff
Director of Design: Louis Klein
Editorial Board: Dale M. Brown, Roberta Conlan,
Ellen Phillips, Gerry Schremp, Donia Ann Steele,
Rosalind Stubenberg, Kit van Tulleken,
Henry Woodhead
Director of Research: Phyllis K. Wise
Director of Photography: John Conrad Weiser

PRESIDENT: William J. Henry
Senior Vice President: Christopher T. Linen
Vice Presidents: Stephen L. Bair, Edward Brash,
Ralph J. Cuomo, Robert A. Ellis, John M. Fahey Jr.,
Juanita T. James, James L. Mercer, Wilhelm R. Saake,
Robert H. Smith, Paul R. Stewart, Leopoldo Toralballa

Editorial Operations
Design: Ellen Robling (assistant director)
Copy Chief: Diane Ullius
Editorial Operations: Caroline A. Boubin (manager)
Production: Celia Beattie
Quality Control: James J. Cox (director)
Library: Louise D. Forstall

Correspondents: Elisabeth Kraemer-Singh (Bonn);
Margot Hapgood, Dorothy Bacon (London); Miriam Hsia
(New York); Maria Vincenza Aloisi, Josephine
du Brusle (Paris); Ann Natanson (Rome).

Library of Congress Cataloguing in Publication Data
Main entry under title:
Fresh ways with poultry.
(Healthy home cooking)
Includes index.
1. Cookery (Poultry) I. Time-Life Books. II. Series.
TX750.F73 1986   641.6'65   85-20886
ISBN 0-8094-5804-7
ISBN 0-8094-5805-5 (lib. bdg.)

For information on and a full description of any Time-Life Books
series, please write:
Reader Information
Time-Life Books
541 North Fairbanks Court
Chicago, Illinois 60611

Time-Life Books Inc. offers a wide range of fine recordings,
including a *Big Bands* series. For subscription information, call
1-800-621-7026, or write TIME-LIFE MUSIC, Time & Life Building,
Chicago, Illinois 60611.

HEALTHY HOME COOKING

SERIES DIRECTOR: Dale M. Brown
Deputy Editor: Barbara Fleming
Series Administrator: Elise Ritter Gibson
Designer: Herbert H. Quarmby
Picture Editor: Sally Collins
Photographer: Renée Comet
Editorial Assistant: Rebecca C. Christoffersen

Editorial Staff for *Fresh Ways with Poultry:*
Text Editor: Allan Fallow
Researcher/Writers: Jean Getlein, Barbara Sause
(principals), Susan Benesch, Scarlet Cheng,
Andrea E. Reynolds, Susan Stuck
Copy Coordinators: Marfé Ferguson, Elizabeth Graham
Picture Coordinator: Linda Yates

Special Contributors: Carol Gvozdich (nutrition analysis),
Nancy Lendved (props)

THE COOKS

ADAM DE VITO began his cooking apprenticeship at L'Auberge
Chez François near Washington, D.C., when he was only 14.
He has worked at Washington's
Le Pavillon restaurant, taught
with cookbook author Mad-
eleine Kamman, and conducted
classes at L'Académie de Cuisine
in Maryland. He developed most
of the recipes in this volume.

HENRY GROSSI, who started
his cooking career with a New
York caterer, earned a Grand
Diplôme at the École de Cuisine
La Varenne in Paris. He then
served as the school's assistant
director and as its North
American business and publications coordinator.

JOHN T. SHAFFER is a graduate
of The Culinary Institute of
America at Hyde Park, New
York. He has had broad experi-
ence as a chef, including five
years at The Four Seasons Hotel
in Washington, D.C., where he
was *chef saucier* at Aux Beaux
Champs restaurant.

THE CONSULTANT

CAROL CUTLER lives in Washington, D.C., and is the
prizewinning author of many cookbooks, including *The
Six-Minute Soufflé and Other Culinary Delights* and *Pâté:
The New Main Course for the 80's.* During the 12 years
she lived in France, she studied at the Cordon Bleu and
the École des Trois Gourmandes, as well as with pri-
vate chefs. She is a member of the Cercle des Gourmettes
and a charter member and past president of Les
Dames d'Escoffier.

THE NUTRITION CONSULTANT

JANET TENNEY has been involved in nutrition and con-
sumer affairs since she received her master's degree in
human nutrition from Columbia University. She is the
manager for developing and implementing nutritional
programs for a major chain of supermarkets in the Washington, D.C., area.

Other Publications:

UNDERSTANDING COMPUTERS
YOUR HOME
THE ENCHANTED WORLD
THE KODAK LIBRARY OF CREATIVE PHOTOGRAPHY
GREAT MEALS IN MINUTES
THE CIVIL WAR
PLANET EARTH
COLLECTOR'S LIBRARY OF THE CIVIL WAR
THE EPIC OF FLIGHT
THE GOOD COOK
THE SEAFARERS
WORLD WAR II
HOME REPAIR AND IMPROVEMENT
THE OLD WEST

This volume is one of a series of illustrated cookbooks
that emphasizes the preparation of healthful dishes for
today's weight-conscious, nutrition-minded eaters.

Roast Gingered Turkey Breast

2 Turkey Transformed 84

3 Updating Some Old Favorites 112

Braised Goose Legs with Shiitake Mushrooms

4 Poultry in the Microwave Oven 126

Techniques 136

Turkey Cutlets with Citrus

Poultry's Boundless Possibilities

Surely one of nature's greatest gifts to cooks the world over is poultry. No food can be treated more variously in the kitchen and brought to the table in more delicious guises; nor is there meat with more innate goodness than that of the two most popular birds — chicken and turkey. When skinned, both are wonderfully low in fat and therefore in calories, yet they are high in protein. Even duck and goose, long considered so rich as to be indulged in only at holidays or other festive occasions, can be eaten year round when measures are taken to relieve them of much of their fat.

This book celebrates the limitless possibilities of poultry. It presents 119 recipes — for sautéing, braising, broiling, baking, roasting and poaching birds. All were evolved in Time-Life Books' test kitchens by experienced cooks and nutritionists seeking ways to prepare poultry so that it has maximum flavor but still meets today's preference for light, healthful food.

In these recipes, the dual goal of nutritional soundness and eating pleasure is achieved in a number of ways. For example, since most of the fat in chicken and turkey is contained in and under the skin, the recipes frequently call for the skin to be removed and steps to be taken to keep the exposed flesh from drying out. Coatings or liquids provide protection in certain cases. In most sauté recipes, salt is sprinkled on the meat during cooking rather than at the outset, when it would draw out juices. In several dishes, vegetables are partially precooked and then added to the meat so that the cooking time can be shortened, further ensuring the meat's tenderness and moistness. Where the skin is essential to the success of a dish, as in a roast, the exuded fat is skimmed from the juices before the preparation of a sauce.

Few ingredients offer more rewards in the cooking of poultry than stock made at home from vegetables, herbs, and poultry trimmings and bones that might otherwise be discarded (trimmings can be frozen and saved until enough have accumulated). Stock serves variously as a moistener, as a cooking medium in braising or poaching poultry, and as a base for sauces. To add extra flavor, even the skin may be incorporated into the stock-

pot, providing the fat is removed later *(recipe, page 9)*. When the strained liquid is allowed to cool, most of the fat will rise to the surface and congeal. It can then be lifted off easily and thrown away — or, in waste-not families, placed outdoors in winter as a cold-weather treat for wild birds.

Homemade stock may be stored safely in the refrigerator for three or four days, or it can be frozen: Pouring it into small plastic containers in premeasured amounts, freezing it, and then drawing upon it as it is needed without having to melt the whole batch can be a boon to the busy cook. Stock may be stored frozen in tightly covered containers for up to six months. Canned broth may be substituted in recipes where stock is used as a moistener; but because much canned broth is excessively salty, a low-sodium product should be used, or any salt that is called for in the recipe should be eliminated or reduced.

In stock's role as a flavor-rich base for sauces, a little cream or butter may be added for enrichment or as a thickening agent — but always judiciously. In sauces where tartness is welcome, yogurt or buttermilk can be included (mixing a little cornstarch with the yogurt will keep it from separating).

How to use this volume

The book is organized simply. The first and by far the largest section is devoted to chicken in all its delicious variety and to the chicken's close relative, the Cornish hen. Chicken is followed by turkey, another bird that lends itself to many diverse and delicious preparations — most of them surprising. For the cook's convenience, these two sections are broken down by cooking method; thus all the sautés appear together, as do the braises, the poaches, and so on. A third section of the book offers recipes for duck, goose, pheasant, quail and squab; it is organized by type of bird. In a final recipe section, several pages deal with the cooking of poultry in the microwave oven. For every recipe in the book, there is a photograph of the actual dish.

The volume also includes instructions for generalized techniques common to a number of the recipes, such as cutting a chicken into parts or boning a breast. These are demonstrated in a series of how-to photographs. Finally, there is a glossary that describes many of the foods and terms in the book.

The recipes treat poultry as a delicate meat that can all too easily spoil and that can all too easily be overcooked. Ideally, poultry should be bought fresh — and the fresher the better. Some cooks have taken to seeking out fresh-killed, free-range chickens, reared as of old on farms where the birds can strut around the barnyard and peck at seeds and other tidbits to their hearts' content. These free-range chickens do have excellent flavor, but they are hard to find and more often than not the birds are sold to restaurants.

Poultry tips

Most poultry available in markets is Grade A. A bird should have a clean skin without blemishes, bruises or pinfeathers. A pliable breastbone and soft, thin skin indicate a bird's youthfulness (skin color, which may range from white to yellow, is of little significance). Chickens are generally packaged with a "sell by" or "use by" date on the label. Sometimes even the freshest of packaged chickens can emit a chickeny odor when unwrapped, but the smell will quickly dissipate; the odor of a spoiled chicken, however, will not go away, and the bird should be returned.

Fresh poultry should be treated carefully to curtail bacterial growth. It should be refrigerated as soon after purchase as possible. If the package contains a large amount of pinkish juices, discard them, rinse the bird under cold running water, and pat it dry. The drying is important, because bacteria thrive in a moist environment. The bird should then be wrapped tightly and stored in the coldest part of the refrigerator at 40° F. or below, but for no longer than two days. (Although refrigeration retards the growth of bacteria, food-spoiling bacteria grow even in the cold.) Cooked poultry can be kept as long as four days, but when covered with a sauce or liquid, it should be kept only one or two days. Poultry should never be cooked partially and then refrigerated: Bacteria will continue to multiply in the raw portions.

Just before poultry is to be used, it should be rinsed and dried. The cavity of a bird intended for stuffing should be washed to flush out any bacteria and remaining bits of organs. The stuffing itself should be inserted cool but not chilled — do not pack it tightly since it will expand — and the bird should be placed in a preheated oven immediately. Cooks should wash their hands in warm, soapy water before and after handling poultry, as well as any knives, cutting boards or countertops used during its preparation to avoid the transference of bacteria to other foods.

Fresh poultry pieces that will be stored longer than a couple of days should be frozen immediately: To avoid freezer burn, re-move the pieces from the store wrapper and rewrap them tightly in a moistureproof, vaporproof material such as freezer paper or heavy aluminum foil. When a fresh whole bird is to be frozen, the giblets should be frozen separately to keep them from spoiling. A whole bird purchased frozen should be kept in its wrapper until ready to use; flash-frozen by the processor to lock in flavor, the bird can be kept for as long as a year at 0° F. or below.

Dealing with frozen poultry

The safest way to thaw frozen poultry is gradually in the refrigerator, where the cold slows the growth of bacteria. But it takes time: 12 to 16 hours for a whole four-pound bird, four to nine hours for pieces. Fresh poultry frozen at home should be used before six months have elapsed to guard against a deterioration in the taste and texture of the meat.

Some of the recipes presented here may be prepared in advance and frozen, but this practice is not recommended unless schedules demand it. The success of the dishes depends on fresh ingredients, and critical flavors will inevitably be lost or distorted when the food is frozen. Certain herbs, for example, seem to relinquish much of their character; such seasonings as garlic, onions, pepper, nutmeg and cloves become more intense. Furthermore, there is little point to freezing the book's many sautés, broils and stir-fries, since they take so little time to cook in the first place. As for the other recipes, most of them have been developed with the exigencies of time in mind, and the dishes themselves are meant to be served immediately, full of aroma and goodness. If, however, any of the dishes are to be frozen, their vegetables should be undercooked, since they will cook still further when they are defrosted and reheated. The dishes should be cooled thoroughly in the refrigerator before being wrapped, labeled, dated and placed in the freezer. And they should be eaten as soon afterward as possible, preferably within the month.

When is the bird done?

How long to cook poultry is, in the end, a matter of personal choice, but the adventurous eater will want to experiment a bit. Too much poultry is rendered dry, tough and tasteless by careless cooking — the "rubber chicken" of the big fund-raising dinner being a case in point. In this book, poultry is cooked respectfully. Chicken and turkey come out moist and tender. Duck breast skinned and sautéed emerges a rosy pink, rich in flavor not unlike that of the best beef, but without beef's calories.

One simple test for doneness is to poke the meat with a finger; it should feel firm but springy to the touch. Another test is to pierce a thigh with the tip of a sharp knife; the juices should run clear (when they are pink, the meat needs further cooking).

The Key to Better Eating

This book, like others in the Healthy Home Cooking series, presents an analysis of nutrients contained in a single serving of each dish, listed beside the recipe itself, as at right. Actual counts for calories, protein, cholesterol, total fat, saturated fat (the kind that increases the body's blood cholesterol), and sodium are given.

Healthy Home Cooking addresses the concerns of today's weight-conscious, health-minded cooks by providing recipes that fall within guidelines set by nutritionists. The secret to eating well, of course, has to do with maintaining a balance of foods in the diet; most Americans consume too much sugar and salt, too much fat and too many calories, even too much of the very nutrient considered the most important of all — protein.

The chart below shows the National Research Council's recommended average daily allowances of calories and protein for healthy men, women and children, along with the council's recommendations for the "safe and adequate" maximum intake of sodium. Although the council has not established similar recommendations for either cholesterol or fat, the chart does include what the National Institutes of Health and the American Heart Association consider the maximum allowable amounts of these in one day's eating by healthy members of the general population.

The volumes in the Healthy Home Cooking series do not purport to be diet books, nor do they focus on health foods. Rather, they express a commonsense approach to cooking that uses salt, sugar, cream, butter and oil in moderation while employing other ingredients that also provide flavor and satisfaction. Herbs, spices, aromatic vegetables, fruits, peels, and juices, wines and vinegars are all used toward this end.

The recipes make no unusual demands. Naturally they call for fresh ingredients, offering substitutes when these are unavailable. (Only the first ingredient is calculated in the nutrient analysis, however.) Most of the

Calories **339**
Protein **30g.**
Cholesterol **125mg.**
Total fat **14g.**
Saturated fat **3g.**
Sodium **236mg.**

ingredients can be found in any well-stocked supermarket; the occasional exception can be bought in specialty shops or ethnic stores.

In Healthy Home Cooking's test kitchens, heavy-bottomed pots and pans are used to guard against burning the food whenever a small amount of oil is used, but nonstick pans could be utilized as well. Both safflower oil and virgin olive oil are favored for sautéing. Safflower was chosen because it is the most highly polyunsaturated vegetable fat available in supermarkets, and polyunsaturated fats reduce blood cholesterol. Virgin olive oil is used because it has a fine fruity flavor lacking in the lesser grade known as "pure." In addition, it is — like all olive oil — high in monounsaturated fats, which do not increase blood cholesterol and, according to recent research, may even lower it. Sometimes both virgin and safflower oils are combined, with the olive oil contributing its fruitiness to the safflower oil. When virgin olive oil is unavailable, "pure" may be substituted.

To help the cook plan ahead effectively, Healthy Home Cooking takes time into account in all of its recipes. While recognizing that everyone cooks at a different speed, and that stoves and ovens differ in temperatures, the series provides approximate "working" and "total" times for every dish. Working time stands for the actual minutes spent on preparation; total time includes unattended cooking time, as well as any other time devoted to marinating, steeping or soaking various ingredients. Since the recipes emphasize fresh foods, they may take a bit longer to prepare than the dishes in "quick and easy" cookbooks that call for canned or packaged products, but the payoff in flavor and often in nutrition should compensate for the little extra time involved.

In order to simplify meal planning, the recipes in this book list accompaniments. These accompaniments are intended only as suggestions, however; cooks should let their imaginations be their guide and come up with ideas of their own to achieve an appealing and sensible balance of foods.

Recommended Dietary Guidelines

		Average Daily Intake		Maximum Daily Intake			
		CALORIES	PROTEIN grams	CHOLESTEROL milligrams	TOTAL FAT grams	SATURATED FAT grams	SODIUM milligrams
Children	7-10	2400	22	240	80	27	1800
Females	11-14	2200	37	220	73	24	2700
	15-18	2100	44	210	70	23	2700
	19-22	2100	44	300	70	23	3300
	23-50	2000	44	300	67	22	3300
	51-75	1800	44	300	60	20	3300
Males	11-14	2700	36	270	90	30	2700
	15-18	2800	56	280	93	31	2700
	19-22	2900	56	300	97	32	3300
	23-50	2700	56	300	90	30	3300
	51-75	2400	56	300	80	27	3300

For whole birds, the most reliable method is to insert a quick-reading meat thermometer in the thickest part of the thigh muscle, taking care that the thermometer does not come into contact with the bone. Turkey, for example, is done when its internal temperature reaches 180° to 185° F. Allowing a large bird to stand at room temperature for about 20 minutes after it finishes roasting will make the meat easier to carve.

Choosing a wine accompaniment

What to drink with poultry is, like the cooking of it, largely a matter of preference. Wine is a pleasant accompaniment to any bird, although beer seems to better complement dishes with a spicy Asian accent, such as the turkey satays on page 99 or the yogurt-baked chicken thighs on page 58. Picking an appropriate wine is harder today than it was a dozen years ago. For one thing, there are more wines to choose from. For another, dishes have become more varied and complex, making the old rule — red wine with red meat, white wine with poultry or fish — obsolete. The new cooking audaciously combines varied foods and flavors and borrows freely from foreign cuisines. The recipes in this book are typical of the new cooking. For interest and flavor, they draw upon a full repertoire of herbs and spices and other savory ingredients, and the finished dishes often are served with light sauces or dressings. Someone seeking to heighten his or her pleasure in the food has an obligation to give careful thought to the selection of a wine to drink with it.

Although there can be no strict rules, the following considerations should be borne in mind when choosing the wine: Take into account the nature of the dish and try to match like with like. If the dish is, for example, the duck breasts with sour apples on page 115, the pink, rich-tasting meat automatically suggests a red wine, while the tart apple seems to call for a tart or slightly acid wine that can hold its own against the fruit's assertiveness. A young Bordeaux or a big Beaujolais such as a Juliénas or a Morgon would make a perfect companion.

The turkey scallopini on page 97 contrasts white breast meat with red and green peppers. A white wine seems in order, but the sweet, somewhat acid flavor of the peppers requires that the wine share these qualities to complement the dish properly. Thus a good choice here would be a California Chenin Blanc or a crisp Alsatian Riesling.

The hearty roast goose with apple-and-red-cabbage stuffing on page 121 demands a full-bodied red wine — perhaps a mature Burgundy or Côtes du Rhône. A simple roast chicken stuffed under the skin with fresh thyme (page 78) can be consumed with any good wine — a young California Zinfandel or Chardonnay or even a Chianti Classico. The beauty of poultry is that it encourages such experimentation.

A Basic Chicken Stock

Makes 2 to 3 quarts
Working time: about 20 minutes
Total time: about 3 hours

4 to 5 lb. uncooked chicken trimmings and bones (preferably wings, necks and backs), the bones cracked with a heavy knife
2 carrots, cut into ½-inch rounds
2 celery stalks, cut into 1-inch pieces
2 large onions, cut in half, one half stuck with 2 cloves
2 sprigs fresh thyme, or ½ tsp. dried thyme leaves
1 or 2 bay leaves
10 to 15 parsley stems
5 whole black peppercorns

Put the trimmings and bones in a heavy stockpot with enough water to cover them by 2 inches. Bring the liquid to a slow boil, skimming off the scum that rises to the surface. Boil for 10 minutes, skimming and adding a little cold water to help precipitate the scum. Add the vegetables, herbs and peppercorns, and submerge them in the liquid. If necessary, add enough additional water to cover the vegetables or bones. Reduce the heat to low and simmer for two to three hours, skimming once more.

Strain the stock and allow it to stand until tepid, then refrigerate it overnight or freeze it long enough for the fat to congeal. Spoon off and discard the layer of fat.

Tightly covered, the stock may safely be kept for three to four days in the refrigerator. Stored in small, well-covered freezer containers, the stock may be kept frozen for up to six months.

EDITOR'S NOTE: *The chicken gizzard and heart may be added to the stock, along with the bird's uncooked skin. Wings and necks — rich in natural gelatin — produce a particularly gelatinous stock, ideal for sauces and jellied dishes.*

Since the recipes in this book contain little salt, cooks may wish to prepare a stock with a more complex flavor. Unpeeled, lightly crushed garlic cloves, dried basil, additional bay leaves or parsley stems — even a sweet potato cut in half — may be used to heighten the flavor of the stock without overwhelming it. Turkey, duck or goose stock may be prepared from the same basic recipe, but the fatty skin of duck or goose should not be used.

1 *Two spatchcocked chickens, topped with Parmesan cheese and garnished with basil, are served with a basil-yogurt sauce and stewed tomatoes (recipe, page 81).*

Chicken: Today's Perfect Meat

Chicken has something to offer everyone — dark and white meat, multiple cooking options, and the ability to marry the flavors of most herbs and spices. Its nutritional credentials are no less compelling: Chicken has fewer calories and is easier to digest than beef, yet a three-ounce serving of boneless broiled chicken breast contains about the same amount of protein as lean beef — 26.3 grams. With its skin removed and any excess visible fat scraped away, chicken becomes even more healthful: It loses at least 40 calories per three-ounce serving. No wonder chicken is fast becoming the most popular meat in America.

Success in preparing the chicken dishes in this book depends partly on choosing the right kind of bird for the recipe at hand. Broilers, often labeled "broiler/fryer" or "fryer" in the market, are about seven weeks old when slaughtered and can weigh anywhere from two and one half to four pounds. Their age and size makes them especially tender. They can be sautéed and roasted, as well as broiled. Roasters, being bigger than broilers, are inevitably older — by five weeks or so — with more fat in and under their skin. Since chicken cannot be roasted easily without skin, the fat can be reduced by first steaming the bird and then putting it immediately into a hot oven; this also helps tenderize the meat. Cut into pieces and skinned, roasters may also be sautéed, broiled, or used for stewing or braising. Capons are male chickens that have been neutered, a procedure that renders them meatier, tenderer and tastier than roasters, but gives them more fat. They are generally brought to market when they reach 15 to 16 weeks and weigh nine to 10 pounds.

The old-fashioned stewing chicken, or "fowl," that for centuries has imparted rich flavor to hearty soups and stews the world over may be 15 or more months in age when marketed, and its flesh will inevitably be stringier than that of younger birds. At the opposite extreme in age and size is the Cornish hen, chicken's smaller but no less succulent relative, which is specified for a number of recipes in the section that follows. Cornish hens are a mere four to five weeks old at slaughtering and vary in weight from one to two pounds. They may be sautéed, roasted or broiled; each bird is often a single portion in itself.

Determining how much chicken to buy for a meal depends on how it is to be cooked and how many people it is supposed to feed. For a whole bird, a half pound works out to about three ounces after cooking and the removal of the skin and bones. As for chicken parts, one half of a whole breast, a whole leg, two drumsticks, two thighs or three wings usually constitute a three-ounce serving, considered an ideal adult portion by nutritionists.

Stir-Fried Minced Chicken on Lettuce Leaves

Serves 6
Working time: about 30 minutes
Total time: about 45 minutes

Calories **277**
Protein **27g.**
Cholesterol **66mg.**
Total fat **13g.**
Saturated fat **2g.**
Sodium **590mg.**

1¼ lb. chicken breast meat, finely chopped
¼ cup dried Chinese mushrooms
1 tbsp. cornstarch
2 tbsp. dry sherry
¼ tsp. salt
1 tsp. Sichuan peppercorns, or ½ tsp. freshly ground black pepper
2 heads iceberg lettuce
3 tbsp. safflower oil
1 tbsp. finely chopped fresh ginger
2 garlic cloves, finely chopped
2 scallions, finely chopped
½ cup chopped water chestnuts
1 cup chopped bamboo shoots
2 oz. boiled ham, finely chopped
3 tbsp. low-sodium soy sauce
2 tsp. dark sesame oil

Soak the mushrooms in a bowl of hot water for 10 minutes. Stir to release any sand, then let them stand in the water for another 20 minutes before draining them. Cut off and discard the stems, slice the mushrooms thinly, and set them aside.

In a bowl, mix the cornstarch and the sherry. Add the salt and the chicken. Combine well and set aside to marinate for at least 15 minutes.

Meanwhile, in a small, heavy-bottomed skillet, toast the peppercorns over medium heat for three to four minutes, shaking the pan frequently. Remove the peppercorns from the pan and crush them with the flat of a knife. Set aside.

Carefully separate the lettuce leaves. Trim them with a sharp knife or scissors to produce 12 cuplike leaves of comparable size. Set aside.

Heat a wok or a large, heavy-bottomed skillet over high heat. Add 2 tablespoons of the safflower oil and swirl the pan to coat its surface. Add the chicken and stir fry until the meat loses its pink hue — two to three minutes. Remove the chicken and set it aside.

Heat the remaining tablespoon of safflower oil over high heat. Add the ginger, garlic, scallions, water chestnuts and bamboo shoots, and stir fry for two minutes. Then add the ham, mushrooms and peppercorns or black pepper, and stir fry for another minute. Toss in the chicken and stir fry until it is heated through. Remove the wok or skillet from the heat and stir in the soy sauce and the sesame oil. Arrange the lettuce leaves on a platter, spoon the mixture onto them and serve. The chicken-filled leaves are all the more delicious eaten with the hands.

SUGGESTED ACCOMPANIMENTS: *steamed rice; bean sprouts.*
EDITOR'S NOTE: *Stir frying is designed to sear meats and cook vegetables quickly, without sacrificing their color, texture or flavor. It must be executed speedily so the meats will not toughen and the vegetables will not wilt.*

Sautéed Chicken Breasts with Livers and Grapes

Serves 4
Working time: about 40 minutes
Total time: about 40 minutes

Calories **295**
Protein **32g.**
Cholesterol **212mg.**
Total fat **11g.**
Saturated fat **3g.**
Sodium **216mg.**

4 chicken breast halves, skinned and boned (about 1 lb.)
1 tsp. unsalted butter
1 tbsp. safflower oil
¼ tsp. salt
freshly ground black pepper
½ cup Madeira
¼ cup finely chopped shallots
½ tsp. mustard seeds, crushed
1 tsp. fresh thyme, or ¼ tsp. dried thyme leaves
¼ lb. chicken livers
¼ lb. seedless grapes (about ¾ cup), cut in half
2 tbsp. sour cream
2 tsp. plain low-fat yogurt
1 tsp. cornstarch, mixed with 1 tbsp. fresh lime juice
1 tbsp. chopped parsley

Heat the butter and 1 teaspoon of the oil in a heavy-bottomed skillet over medium-high heat. Cook the chicken breasts on one side until they are lightly browned — about four minutes. Turn the pieces over and sprinkle them with the salt and pepper. Cook for three minutes on the second side, then remove the breasts, place on a heated platter, and set aside.

Pour the Madeira into the skillet and simmer to reduce it by half — about three minutes. Add the shallots, mustard seeds and thyme, and simmer for two or three minutes more. Pour the sauce over the chicken, scraping out the pan deposits along with it.

Wipe the skillet with a paper towel. Heat the remaining 2 teaspoons of oil in the pan over medium-high heat, and sauté the chicken livers, turning occasionally, until they brown — about six minutes. Reduce the heat to low, return the chicken breasts and their sauce to the pan, and add the grapes. Stir the sour cream and yogurt into the cornstarch-lime juice mixture, then pour it into the pan. Simmer until the chicken is cooked through — about five minutes. Garnish with the parsley and serve immediately.

SUGGESTED ACCOMPANIMENTS: *rice pilaf; green beans.*

Chicken Cutlets with Summer Herbs and Tomato Sauce

Serves 4
Working time: about 30 minutes
Total time: about 30 minutes

Calories **278**
Protein **30g.**
Cholesterol **71mg.**
Total fat **10g.**
Saturated fat **2g.**
Sodium **327mg.**

4 chicken breast halves, boned and skinned (about 1 lb.), pounded to about ½-inch thickness
1 garlic clove, finely chopped
2 large tomatoes, peeled, seeded and coarsely chopped
1 tbsp. virgin olive oil
½ cup unsalted chicken stock
¾ tsp. tarragon vinegar
1 tbsp. each of finely chopped fresh tarragon, basil and parsley, mixed, plus sprigs for garnishing
¼ tsp. salt
¼ tsp. freshly ground white pepper
½ cup dry bread crumbs
2 egg whites
1 tbsp. safflower oil

To prepare the sauce, cook the garlic and tomatoes in the olive oil over medium-high heat in a small saucepan, stirring occasionally, until soft — about five minutes. Add the chicken stock, the vinegar and 2 tablespoons of the herb mixture, and bring to a boil. Reduce the heat, cover and simmer for five minutes. Purée the sauce in a food processor or blender and return it to the pan to keep warm.

Meanwhile, sprinkle the salt and pepper over the breasts. Mix the remaining tablespoon of herbs with the bread crumbs on a large plate. In a small bowl, whisk the egg whites vigorously and dip the breasts in the whites, then in the bread-crumb mixture.

Heat the safflower oil in a large, heavy-bottomed skillet over medium-high heat and sauté the chicken on one side until lightly brown — about three minutes. Turn the breasts, cover the skillet loosely, and sauté until they feel firm but springy to the touch — about four minutes more. Transfer the breasts to a heated platter and spoon the sauce over them. Garnish with sprigs of herbs.

SUGGESTED ACCOMPANIMENT: *corn on the cob.*

Chicken Breasts Sautéed with Cilantro

Serves 4
Working time: about 30 minutes
Total time: about 30 minutes

Calories **203**
Protein **29g.**
Cholesterol **77mg.**
Total fat **7g.**
Saturated fat **2g.**
Sodium **233mg.**

4 chicken breast halves, skinned and boned (about 1 lb.)
1 tbsp. safflower oil
freshly ground black pepper
¼ tsp. salt
⅓ cup plain low-fat yogurt
2 tbsp. light cream
1 tsp. cornstarch, mixed with 1 tbsp. water
¾ cup unsalted chicken stock
2 tbsp. fresh lemon juice
2 garlic cloves, finely chopped
2 tbsp. finely chopped shallot
1 small tomato, peeled, seeded and chopped
⅓ cup stemmed cilantro, coarsely chopped, 4 leaves reserved for a garnish

In a heavy-bottomed skillet, heat the oil over medium-high heat. Sauté the chicken breasts on one side for five minutes, then turn them and sprinkle with the pepper and ⅛ teaspoon of the salt. Sauté on the second side until firm but springy to the touch — about four minutes. Transfer the chicken to a heated platter and keep it warm.

In a small bowl, stir the yogurt and cream into the cornstarch mixture. Put the stock and lemon juice in the skillet; add the garlic and shallot, reduce the heat to low, and simmer for 30 seconds. Stir in the tomato, the yogurt mixture and the remaining ⅛ teaspoon of salt. Cook over low heat for one minute, then add the cilantro. Pour the sauce over the chicken. Garnish each breast with a fresh cilantro leaf if desired.

SUGGESTED ACCOMPANIMENT: *sautéed zucchini.*

Sautéed Chicken Breasts with Raspberry Sauce

Serves 4
Working time: about 30 minutes
Total time: about 40 minutes

Calories **226**
Protein **27g.**
Cholesterol **80mg.**
Total fat **7g.**
Saturated fat **3g.**
Sodium **153mg.**

4 chicken breast halves, skinned and boned (about 1 lb.)
⅛ tsp. salt
freshly ground black pepper
1 tsp. honey
1 tbsp. raspberry vinegar
1 tbsp. unsalted butter
½ cup dry white wine
1 shallot, finely chopped
¾ cup fresh raspberries
1 cup unsalted chicken stock
mint sprigs, for garnish (optional)

Sprinkle the chicken breasts with the salt and pepper and put them on a plate. Stir the honey into the raspberry vinegar and mix well. Dribble this mixture over the breasts and allow them to marinate for 15 minutes.

Preheat the oven to 200° F. In a heavy-bottomed skillet, melt the butter over medium-high heat, and sauté the breasts until golden — about four minutes on each side. Transfer the chicken to a serving platter and put the platter in the oven to keep warm. Add the wine and shallot to the skillet. Reduce the liquid until it barely coats the pan — there should be about 2 tablespoons. Reserve 12 of the raspberries for a garnish. Add the stock and the remaining raspberries and reduce by half, to about ¾ cup. Purée the mixture in a food processor or blender, then strain it through a fine sieve. Return the sauce to the skillet and bring it to a boil. Spoon it over the chicken and garnish with the reserved raspberries and the mint sprigs, if desired.

SUGGESTED ACCOMPANIMENTS: *green peas; steamed rice.*

Chicken with Peanuts and Ginger Sauce

Serves 6
Working time: about 20 minutes
Total time: about 2 hours and 20 minutes

Calories **261**
Protein **30g.**
Cholesterol **71mg.**
Total fat **12g.**
Saturated fat **3g.**
Sodium **200mg.**

1½ lb. chicken breast meat, cut into ½-inch cubes
½ cup dry white wine
¼ cup fresh ginger, finely chopped
1 garlic clove, crushed
¼ tsp. salt
freshly ground black pepper
1 cup unsalted chicken stock
2 tbsp. peanut butter
1 tsp. tomato paste (optional)
2 scallions, julienned
⅓ cup peanuts, crushed with a rolling pin
1 tbsp. safflower oil

Make a marinade of the wine, ginger, garlic, salt and pepper, and let the chicken stand in it for two hours.

Near the end of the marinating time, prepare the sauce. Pour the stock into a small saucepan and whisk in the peanut butter and the tomato paste, if desired. Add the scallions and simmer over low heat, uncovered, for two minutes. Remove the saucepan from the heat and set it aside.

Remove the cubes from the marinade and set them aside. Strain the marinade and add it to the sauce. Return the mixture to a simmer and cook over low heat, stirring occasionally, until the sauce is thick enough to coat the back of a spoon — about four minutes. Remove the pan from the heat.

Roll the chicken cubes in the crushed peanuts, sparsely coating the cubes. Heat the oil in a heavy-bottomed skillet over high heat. When the oil is hot but not smoking, add the chicken cubes and lightly brown them, stirring gently to keep intact as much of the peanut coating as possible — about three minutes. Re-move the skillet from the heat and allow the chicken to finish cooking as it rests in the hot pan — about two minutes more. Transfer the chicken to a warmed plat-ter and pour the sauce over it just before serving.

SUGGESTED ACCOMPANIMENTS: *steamed rice; fried bananas; cucumber salad.*

Sautéed Chicken with Mustard, Caraway Seeds and Chervil

Serves 4
Working time: about 1 hour
Total time: about 1 hour

Calories **442**
Protein **30g.**
Cholesterol **105mg.**
Total fat **18g.**
Saturated fat **8g.**
Sodium **374mg.**

4 chicken breast halves, boned and skinned (about 1 lb.), pounded to ½-inch thickness
⅛ tsp. salt
freshly ground black pepper
3 tbsp. Dijon mustard
⅓ cup plain low-fat yogurt
2 tsp. caraway seeds
5 tbsp. chopped fresh chervil or parsley
1 cup dry bread crumbs
2 tbsp. unsalted butter
1 tbsp. safflower oil
3 tart green apples, cored and cut into ¼-inch slices
2 tbsp. aquavit or kümmel (optional)
½ cup unfiltered apple cider
1 tbsp. fresh lemon juice
¼ cup heavy cream

Sprinkle the pounded breasts with the salt and pepper.

In a small bowl, whisk together the mustard, yo-gurt, caraway seeds and 4 tablespoons of the chervil or parsley. Generously coat the breasts with the mix-ture, then place them in the bread crumbs and pat on the crumbs evenly. Chill for at least 10 minutes, or for up to an hour.

Once the breasts have been chilled, heat 1 table-spoon of the butter and the oil in a large heavy-bottomed skillet over medium heat. Place the breasts in the pan and sauté, turning once, until the crumbs are golden — six to eight minutes.

Heat the remaining tablespoon of butter in a heavy-bottomed skillet over medium heat. Toss in the apple slices and cook them for four to five minutes, turning the slices occasionally. Add the aquavit or kümmel, if using, and simmer to evaporate — one to two minutes. Add the cider, the lemon juice and more pepper, and simmer for three to four minutes. Push the apples to one side of the skillet and whisk in the cream. Cook for two minutes more.

To serve, place the chicken on a heated platter and, using a slotted spoon to lift the apple slices from the pan, arrange the slices around the breasts. Continue simmering the sauce until it thickens slightly — two to three minutes. Pour the sauce over the chicken and apples and garnish with the remaining tablespoon of chervil or parsley. Serve immediately.

SUGGESTED ACCOMPANIMENT: *mashed turnips or rutabaga.*

Chicken Breasts Stuffed with Garlic and Carrots

Serves 4
Working time: about 45 minutes
Total time: about 1 hour

Calories **244**
Protein **28g.**
Cholesterol **73mg.**
Total fat **9g.**
Saturated fat **2g.**
Sodium **362mg.**

4 chicken breast halves, skinned and boned (about 1 lb.)
1 tbsp. virgin olive oil
24 to 32 garlic cloves, peeled
½ tsp. salt
1 large carrot, cut into 12 strips ¼ inch thick and 4 inches long
2 tbsp. fresh rosemary leaves
1 tsp. safflower oil
freshly ground black pepper
½ cup unsalted chicken stock
¼ cup dry white wine
1 shallot, finely chopped

Heat the olive oil in a heavy-bottomed skillet over low heat. Slowly cook the garlic cloves in the olive oil, stirring occasionally, for 20 minutes.

Sprinkle the garlic cloves with ⅛ teaspoon of the salt and continue cooking until they turn golden brown all over — about 10 minutes more. Remove the cloves with a slotted spoon and set them aside. Do not discard the oil in the skillet.

While the garlic is browning, prepare the carrots and the chicken. Blanch the carrot strips in boiling water until tender — about four minutes — then drain them and set them aside. Lay the chicken breasts on a cutting board, their smooth sides facing down. Along the thinner long edge of each breast, make a horizontal slit and cut nearly through to the opposite side. Open each breast so that it forms two flaps hinged at the center. Sprinkle the rosemary and ¼ teaspoon of the salt over the flaps. Arrange three carrot strips on the larger flap of each breast, and distribute the garlic cloves between the carrot strips. Fold the top flaps over the bottoms, align their edges, and press the breasts closed as nearly as possible.

Add the safflower oil to the oil in the skillet and turn

the heat to medium high. When the oil is hot, put the stuffed breasts in the pan and sauté them on one side until they are browned — about five minutes. Turn the breasts gently and sprinkle them with the remaining ⅛ teaspoon of salt and the pepper. Cook the breasts on the second side until they feel firm but springy to the touch — five to seven minutes more. Carefully remove the breasts from the skillet and place them on a warmed serving platter.

Prepare the sauce by stirring the stock, wine and shallot into the skillet to deglaze it. Stir frequently until the sauce is reduced by half, to about ⅓ cup. Pour some sauce over each breast and serve immediately.

SUGGESTED ACCOMPANIMENT: *snow peas with lemon butter.*

Chicken Riesling

Serves 4
Working time: about 30 minutes
Total time: about 1 hour

Calories **310**
Protein **27g.**
Cholesterol **79mg.**
Total fat **11g.**
Saturated fat **3g.**
Sodium **366mg.**

4 chicken breast halves, skinned and boned (about 1 lb.)
freshly ground black pepper
½ tsp. salt
1 tbsp. safflower oil
1 tbsp. unsalted butter
2 tbsp. finely chopped shallots
1 cup thinly sliced mushrooms
1 ½ cups Riesling wine
1 tbsp. chopped fresh tarragon, or 1 tsp. dried tarragon
1 ¼ cups unsalted chicken stock
2 tsp. cornstarch
¾ cup seedless red grapes, halved

Preheat the oven to 200° F.

Sprinkle the chicken with the pepper and ¼ teaspoon of the salt. Heat the oil over medium-high heat in a large, heavy-bottomed skillet. Sauté the pieces in the oil until brown — about five minutes on each side. Transfer the chicken to a platter and cover it with foil.

Add the butter, shallots and mushrooms to the skillet, sprinkle with ⅛ teaspoon of the remaining salt, and sauté until the shallots soften — two to three minutes. With a slotted spoon, transfer the mushrooms to the platter with the chicken, and keep it warm in the oven. Add all but ¼ cup of the Riesling to the skillet along with the tarragon, and reduce the liquid to about ¼ cup. Pour in the stock and reduce by half, to about ¾ cup. Mix the cornstarch with the remaining ¼ cup of wine. Reduce the heat so that the sauce simmers, and stir in the cornstarch mixture and the remaining ⅛ teaspoon of salt. Add the grapes and cook for two minutes. Arrange some of the mushroom mixture on each breast half, and pour the sauce over all.

SUGGESTED ACCOMPANIMENTS: *garlic bread; red leaf lettuce salad.*

Chicken, Eggplant and Tomato Sauté

Serves 4
Working time: about 45 minutes
Total time: about 1 hour

Calories **370**
Protein **30g.**
Cholesterol **75mg.**
Total fat **19g.**
Saturated fat **4g.**
Sodium **207mg.**

4 chicken breast halves, skinned and boned (about 1 lb.)
2 small eggplants, sliced in ⅜-inch-thick rounds
1 tsp. unsalted butter
4 tbsp. virgin olive oil
freshly ground black pepper
¼ tsp. salt
¼ cup dry sherry
2 tbsp. fresh lemon juice
1 tsp. fresh thyme, or ¼ tsp. dried thyme leaves

1 oz. dried mushrooms, rinsed and soaked for one hour in 1 cup warm water, the remaining water strained through doubled cheesecloth to remove grit and reserved
3 large ripe tomatoes, peeled, sliced in ¾-inch-thick rounds, and placed on paper towels to drain
1 tbsp. red wine vinegar
2 garlic cloves, finely chopped
2 scallions, trimmed and finely chopped

In a large saucepan, bring 2 quarts of water to a boil. Blanch the eggplant slices a few at a time in the boiling water for 30 seconds. Remove them with a slotted spoon and drain them on paper towels.

Heat the butter and 1 tablespoon of the oil in a heavy-bottomed skillet over medium-high heat. Sauté the chicken breasts on one side until they brown — about four minutes. Turn them over and sprinkle them with the pepper and ⅛ teaspoon of the salt. Reduce

the heat to low and cook for two minutes. Then add the sherry, lemon juice, thyme and ¼ cup of the water in which the mushrooms soaked. Simmer, covered, until the pieces feel firm but springy to the touch — about five minutes. Remove the pan from the heat and set it aside.

Preheat the oven to 200° F. Heat 1 tablespoon of the remaining oil in a large skillet over medium-high heat. Sauté one third of the eggplant slices in a single layer until golden brown, turning them once. Repeat the process twice more with the remaining eggplant, adding ½ tablespoon of the oil to the skillet before each batch. Cover the bottom of an ovenproof serving dish with the slices.

Heat the remaining tablespoon of oil in the skillet over medium-high heat. Sprinkle the tomato slices with the remaining ⅛ teaspoon of salt and sauté them until softened — about two minutes on the first side and one to two minutes on the second, depending on the ripeness of the tomatoes.

Arrange the tomatoes on top of the eggplant. Remove the chicken pieces from their liquid and layer them on top. Put the dish in the oven to keep warm while you make the sauce.

Bring the liquid in the heavy-bottomed skillet to a simmer over medium heat, then add the mushrooms and the remaining mushroom liquid along with the vinegar, garlic and half of the chopped scallions. Simmer the mixture over low heat until it is reduced by half — about 10 minutes. Spoon this sauce over the chicken, then sprinkle with the remaining chopped scallions and serve at once.

SUGGESTED ACCOMPANIMENT: *Bibb lettuce salad.*

Chicken Paprika with Yogurt

Serves 4
Working time: about 45 minutes
Total time: about 1 hour

Calories **473**
Protein **46g.**
Cholesterol **143mg.**
Total fat **26g.**
Saturated fat **9g.**
Sodium **328mg.**

one 3 lb. chicken, cut into serving pieces, the legs and breast halves skinned
2 tbsp. safflower oil
¼ tsp. salt
1½ cups finely chopped onions
1 garlic clove, finely chopped
1 cup unsalted chicken stock
2 tbsp. paprika
¾ cup plain low-fat yogurt
¾ cup sour cream

In a large, heavy-bottomed skillet, heat the oil over medium-high heat. Add as many chicken pieces as will fit without crowding, and sauté them on one side until brown — about four minutes. Turn the pieces, sprinkle them with the salt, and sauté until the second sides brown — three to four minutes more. Transfer the chicken to a plate. Repeat with the remaining pieces.

Reduce the heat to medium low and add the onions and garlic to the oil remaining in the skillet. Cook, stirring occasionally, until the onions turn translucent — about 10 minutes. Stir in the chicken stock and the paprika, and bring the liquid to a simmer.

Return all of the chicken pieces to the pan, reduce the heat to low, and cover. Simmer until the juices run clear when a thigh is pierced with the tip of a sharp knife — about 25 minutes. Transfer the chicken to a heated platter and cover with foil to keep warm.

Skim any fat from the liquid in the skillet. Bring the liquid to a boil over medium-high heat and reduce the stock to about ½ cup — three to four minutes. In a small bowl, whisk together the yogurt and sour cream. Stir in a little of the cooking liquid, then reduce the heat to low and whisk the yogurt mixture into the pan. Cook for one minute, then pour the sauce over the chicken and serve immediately.

SUGGESTED ACCOMPANIMENTS: *egg noodles; green peas.*

Chicken Breasts with Tarragon and Tomato

Serves 4
Working time: about 30 minutes
Total time: about 2 hours and 30 minutes

Calories **227**
Protein **27g.**
Cholesterol **90mg.**
Total fat **10g.**
Saturated fat **5g.**
Sodium **214mg.**

4 chicken breast halves, skinned and boned (about 1 lb.)
½ cup buttermilk
1 tbsp. fresh lime or lemon juice
1 tbsp. fresh tarragon leaves, or 1 tsp. dried tarragon
1 tbsp. unsalted butter
¼ tsp. salt
2 tomatoes, peeled, seeded and finely chopped
1 shallot, finely chopped
finely ground black pepper
½ cup light cream

In a wide, shallow bowl, combine the buttermilk, lime or lemon juice, and half of the tarragon. Marinate the chicken in this mixture for two hours or overnight. Remove the chicken from the marinade, gently wiping off as much liquid as possible with your fingers.

In a heavy-bottomed skillet, heat the butter over medium heat. Cook the chicken breasts on one side for five minutes. Turn the pieces over, sprinkle them with the salt, and cook for five minutes more. Remove them from the pan and keep them warm.

In the same skillet, cook the tomatoes, shallot, pepper and the remaining tarragon over medium heat until the tomato liquid evaporates — about three minutes. Stir in the cream, reduce the heat to low, and simmer for one minute, stirring. Arrange the breasts on a serving platter and pour the sauce over them just before serving.

SUGGESTED ACCOMPANIMENTS: *julienned carrots; steamed zucchini.*

Stir-Fried Chicken with Broccoli, Red Onions and Cashew Nuts

Serves 4
Working time: about 25 minutes
Total time: about 35 minutes

Calories **352**
Protein **27g.**
Cholesterol **54mg.**
Total fat **20g.**
Saturated fat **3g.**
Sodium **519mg.**

3 chicken breast halves (about ¾ lb.), skinned, boned and sliced into strips about ⅓ inch wide by 3 inches long
½ tsp. salt
¾ tsp. freshly ground white pepper
1¼ tbsp. peanut oil
3 tbsp. safflower oil
5 fresh ginger slices, crushed with the flat of a large knife blade or lightly pounded to just loosen the fibers
5 large garlic cloves, crushed

2 cups broccoli pieces, florets left whole, the stems trimmed and thinly sliced diagonally
2 carrots, thinly sliced diagonally
4 to 6 water chestnuts, sliced (optional)
1 small red onion, chopped into 1-inch squares
2 tbsp. unsalted cashew nuts
3 scallions, sliced diagonally
½ cup unsalted chicken stock
2 tsp. cornstarch, mixed with 1 tbsp. low-sodium soy sauce and 1 tbsp. dry sherry
¼ tsp. dark sesame oil

In a bowl, sprinkle the chicken strips with ¼ teaspoon of the salt and ½ teaspoon of the pepper; stir well.

Heat a wok or a large, deep, heavy-bottomed skillet over medium-high heat. Meanwhile, blend the peanut oil and the safflower oil in a small bowl. When the wok or skillet is hot to the touch, slowly pour in 2 table- ▶

spoons of the blended oil so that it evenly coats the entire cooking surface.

To flavor the oil, stir fry the ginger and garlic for about 30 seconds. Then add the chicken strips and stir fry them in the flavored oil, tossing frequently, until the meat turns white — about three minutes.

Discard the ginger and garlic. Transfer the chicken to a plate and set it aside; do not discard the oil remaining in the pan.

Pour an additional tablespoon of the blended oil into the wok or skillet. Add the broccoli and carrot pieces, sprinkle them with the remaining salt and pepper, and stir fry until the oil has coated all the pieces — one to two minutes. Pour in the remaining tablespoon of blended oil, then add the water chestnuts, if you are using them, the onion, cashews and two thirds of the scallions. Stir fry these with the other vegetables for one to two minutes more.

Return the chicken to the wok or skillet and stir fry the chicken and vegetables together. Push the contents to the sides and pour the stock into the center. Stir the cornstarch mixture into the stock and heat until the liquid boils and thickens. Redistribute the chicken and vegetables in the sauce and stir to coat all the pieces evenly — one to two minutes. Add the sesame oil and stir well.

Serve the dish with the remaining sliced scallions sprinkled over the top.

SUGGESTED ACCOMPANIMENT: *oriental noodles.*

EDITOR'S NOTE: *Stir frying is designed to sear meats and cook vegetables quickly, without sacrificing their color, texture or flavor. It must be executed speedily so the meats will not toughen and the vegetables will not wilt.*

Sautéed Chicken Breasts with Apricots, Bourbon and Pecans

Serves 4
Working time: about 30 minutes
Total time: about 8 hours

Calories **404**
Protein **29g.**
Cholesterol **73mg.**
Total fat **11g.**
Saturated fat **2g.**
Sodium **250mg.**

4 chicken breast halves, skinned and boned (about 1 lb.)
½ lb. dried apricots
⅓ cup bourbon
¾ cup unsalted chicken stock
1 tsp. unsalted butter
1 tsp. safflower oil
¼ tsp. salt
freshly ground black pepper
1 shallot, finely chopped
1 tsp. tomato paste
2 tsp. grainy mustard
¼ cup pecans, toasted in a 350 ° F. oven, then crushed with a rolling pin
1 scallion, cut into 2-inch-long pieces and thinly sliced

Marinate the apricots in the bourbon and ¼ cup of the stock for eight hours or overnight. Alternatively, bring the bourbon and ¼ cup of the stock to a boil, then turn off the heat and steep the apricots in the liquid until they soften — about 10 minutes.

Heat the butter and the oil in a heavy-bottomed skillet over medium-high heat. Sauté the chicken breasts on one side until lightly colored — about four minutes. Turn them over and sprinkle with the salt and pepper. Sauté them on the second side for four minutes. Drain the bourbon and stock from the apricots, and pour it over the chicken. Add the remaining ½ cup of stock, reduce the heat to low, and cook until the chicken feels firm but springy to the touch — about five minutes. Transfer the chicken to a plate and cover with aluminum foil to keep it warm.

Add the apricots and shallot to the skillet and simmer for two minutes. Whisk in the tomato paste and the mustard and simmer the sauce for three minutes, stirring occasionally. Return the breasts to the skillet for a minute or two to heat them through.

Arrange the chicken and the apricots on a warmed serving platter. Spoon the sauce over the chicken and sprinkle with the pecans and scallion.

SUGGESTED ACCOMPANIMENT: *steamed Swiss chard.*

Stir-Fried Chicken with Red Cabbage and Chilies

Serves 4
Working time: about 45 minutes
Total time: about 45 minutes

Calories **266**
Protein **23g.**
Cholesterol **54mg.**
Total fat **10g.**
Saturated fat **1g.**
Sodium **353mg.**

3 chicken breast halves, skinned and boned (about ¾ lb.), cut into ½-inch-wide strips
¼ cup pitted and finely chopped prunes
2 garlic cloves, finely chopped
1 to 2 large dried red chili peppers, seeded and cut into very thin strips, or ½ to 1 tsp. crushed red pepper
2 tbsp. safflower oil
⅓ lb. fresh very thin green beans
1 tbsp. low-sodium soy sauce
1 small head red cabbage, deribbed and cut into 2-inch-long strips
¼ tsp. salt
7 scallions, trimmed, halved lengthwise and cut into 2-inch-long strips

Combine the prunes, garlic, chilies or crushed red pepper, and ½ tablespoon of the oil in a large, shallow dish. Add the chicken and marinate for at least 30 minutes, turning occasionally to coat the meat. Blanch the green beans for one minute in 2 cups of boiling water. Refresh the beans under cold running water, place them in a bowl, and add the soy sauce. Set aside to marinate, turning occasionally to coat the beans.

Heat a wok or large, heavy-bottomed skillet over high heat. Pour in an additional tablespoon of oil and

stir fry the cabbage with the salt until the cabbage wilts — about three minutes. Add the beans with the soy sauce and half the scallions. Continue stir frying for three minutes, stirring and tossing. Empty the wok or skillet into a large bowl.

Return the pan to the heat. Pour in the remaining ½ tablespoon of oil and immediately add the chicken and its marinade along with the rest of the scallions. Reduce the heat to medium high and stir and toss until the chicken is cooked — about four minutes. Add the cabbage mixture, mix well, and serve immediately.

SUGGESTED ACCOMPANIMENTS: *yellow rice; firm tofu sautéed with soy sauce.*

EDITOR'S NOTE: *Stir frying is designed to sear meats and cook vegetables quickly, without sacrificing their color, texture or flavor. It must be executed speedily so the meats will not toughen and the vegetables will not wilt.*

Chilies — A Cautionary Note

Both dried and fresh hot chilies should be handled with care. Their flesh and seeds contain volatile oils that can make skin tingle and cause eyes to burn. Rubber gloves offer protection — but the cook should still be careful not to touch the face, lips or eyes when working with chilies.

Soaking fresh chilies in cold, salted water for an hour will remove some of their fire. If canned chilies are substituted for fresh ones, they should be rinsed in cold water in order to eliminate as much of the brine used to preserve them as possible.

Poached Chicken with Fennel

Serves 6
Working time: about 30 minutes
Total time: about 1 hour

Calories **338**
Protein **29g.**
Cholesterol **96mg.**
Total fat **11g.**
Saturated fat **4g.**
Sodium **515mg.**

6 chicken legs, skinned
1 tsp. black peppercorns
2 garlic cloves, peeled
1 cup anis or other licorice-flavored liqueur
3 cups unsalted chicken stock
1 onion, thinly sliced
½ tsp. fennel seed
1 tsp. salt
2 large fennel bulbs, the tough outer layer and feathery green tops trimmed and reserved, the bulbs cut lengthwise into 6 pieces
1 celery stalk, trimmed, cut into ¼-inch-wide strips about 3 inches long
1 bay leaf
2 large lettuce leaves, preferably romaine
½ lb. baby carrots, tops removed, peeled
1 tbsp. unsalted butter
freshly ground black pepper

Crush the peppercorns and the garlic with a mortar and pestle and mash them into a paste. Spread the paste over each chicken leg.

Bring the liqueur to a boil in a large, heavy-bottomed casserole. Add the chicken legs and turn them to coat them with the liqueur. Add the stock, onion, fennel seed and salt; if necessary, pour in enough water or additional stock to just cover the chicken. Return the liquid to a boil. Reduce the heat to medium low and simmer for 15 minutes.

Meanwhile, make a bouquet garni: Wrap the tough outer layer and trimmings from the fennel, the celery strips and the bay leaf in the lettuce leaves, and tie the bundle with butcher's twine. Submerge the bouquet garni in the poaching liquid.

At the end of the 15 minutes, add the fennel pieces, pressing them into the liquid. Cover the skillet and simmer for five minutes more. Add the carrots and continue cooking, uncovered, until the juices run clear when a thigh is pierced with the tip of a sharp knife — seven to 10 minutes. Transfer the chicken and vegetables to a warmed serving platter.

To make the sauce, reduce the poaching liquid over high heat to about 1¼ cups. Remove and discard the bouquet garni. Whisk the butter and some pepper into

the sauce and pour it over the legs and vegetables; garnish them, if you like, with the feathery fennel tops.

SUGGESTED ACCOMPANIMENT: *sautéed onions and potatoes.*

Poached Chicken Strips in Gingered Orange Sauce

Serves 6
Working time: about 45 minutes
Total time: 1 hour and 30 minutes

Calories **180**
Protein **20g.**
Cholesterol **54mg.**
Total fat **5g.**
Saturated fat **2g.**
Sodium **185mg.**

4 chicken breast halves, skinned and boned (about 1 lb.), cut into ½-inch-wide strips
¼ tsp. salt
freshly ground black pepper
1 cup fresh orange juice
3 cups unsalted chicken stock
1½- to 2-inch piece fresh ginger (¾ to 1 oz.), peeled and cut into chunks
2 navel oranges, the zest julienned and the flesh segmented
¼ tsp. aromatic bitters
1 tsp. bourbon
2 tbsp. cream cheese
1 tbsp. cornstarch

Put the chicken strips in a shallow dish and sprinkle them with ⅛ teaspoon of the salt and some pepper. Pour in the orange juice. Turn the pieces to coat them with the juice. Cover the dish with plastic wrap and refrigerate for one hour.

Lift the chicken strips out of the marinade and set them aside. To make the poaching liquid, pour the marinade into a large saucepan or skillet. Add 2 cups of the stock, the remaining ⅛ teaspoon of salt and some pepper. Squeeze each ginger chunk through a garlic press into the pan, scraping the paste from the outside bottom of the press into the pot and then turning the press over to add the juices. Bring the liquid to a boil, reduce the heat, cover, and simmer for four minutes. Remove the pan from the heat and let the ginger steep in the poaching liquid for 15 minutes.

While the ginger is steeping, put the julienned zest in a small saucepan. Cover the zest with ½ cup of the stock, the bitters and the bourbon. Cook briskly over medium-high heat until almost all the liquid has evaporated, and set the pan aside. In another small saucepan, pour the remaining ½ cup of stock over the orange segments; cover and set aside.

Return the poaching liquid to a boil. Add the chicken strips and reduce the heat to medium. Simmer the

liquid until the chicken feels firm but springy to the touch — about one minute. Remove the chicken with a slotted spoon and set it in the center of a warmed serving platter.

In a small bowl, soften the cream cheese with the back of a spoon. Stir in the cornstarch. Pour about ½ cup of the hot poaching liquid into the bowl and whisk well. Add another cup of the poaching liquid, then pour the contents of the bowl back into the poaching liquid and cook over medium heat, whisking, until the sauce thickens slightly — two or three minutes.

Heat the orange segments in the chicken stock. Spoon some sauce over the chicken strips and garnish them with the julienned zest. Lift the orange segments out of the stock and arrange them around the chicken. Pass the remaining sauce separately.

SUGGESTED ACCOMPANIMENT: *kasha cooked in chicken stock with sliced mushrooms.*

and fasten each roll lengthwise with a small skewer.

Heat the oil in a heavy-bottomed skillet over medium heat and gently sauté the rolls, turning them, until golden — about four minutes. Remove the chicken and pour the sauce into the skillet, stirring, being sure to scrape up any brown bits from the bottom. Return the chicken to the skillet, cover loosely, and simmer for eight minutes, turning once.

Transfer the chicken to a heated platter and remove the skewers. Pour the sauce over the rolls and serve immediately.

SUGGESTED ACCOMPANIMENT: *steamed rice tossed with green peas and sautéed mushrooms.*

Poached Chicken with Black-Bean Onion Sauce

THE FERMENTED BLACK BEANS CALLED FOR IN THIS RECIPE ARE AVAILABLE AT STORES WHERE ASIAN FOODS ARE SOLD.

Serves 4
Working time: about 30 minutes
Total time: about 1 hour and 30 minutes

Calories **486**
Protein **45g.**
Cholesterol **126mg.**
Total fat **18g.**
Saturated fat **4g.**
Sodium **235mg.**

one 3-lb. chicken, trussed
2 tbsp. safflower oil
3 onions, sliced
1 tbsp. flour
2 tsp. fermented black beans, rinsed well
2 garlic cloves, finely chopped
1 cup dry white wine
3 to 4 cups unsalted beef stock
2 tbsp. brandy
1 small potato, peeled and cut into chunks
freshly ground black pepper
1 tbsp. unsalted butter, cut into pieces (optional)

Red-Pepper and Chicken Spirals

Serves 4
Working time: about 30 minutes
Total time: about 45 minutes

Calories **251**
Protein **28g.**
Cholesterol **72mg.**
Total fat **11g.**
Saturated fat **2g.**
Sodium **533mg.**

4 chicken breast halves, skinned, boned, the long triangular fillets removed and reserved for another use, lightly pounded to ¼-inch thickness
¼ tsp. salt
½ tsp. crushed Sichuan peppercorns, or ¼ tsp. crushed black peppercorns
3 scallions, blanched for 30 seconds, drained, cooled, patted dry, and halved lengthwise
1 cucumber, peeled, halved lengthwise, seeded, cut into ¼-inch-wide strips, blanched for 30 seconds, drained, cooled and patted dry
1 sweet red pepper, seeded, deribbed, cut into ½-inch strips, blanched for 2 minutes, drained and patted dry
2 tbsp. safflower oil
Mirin sauce
3 tbsp. low-sodium soy sauce
1 tbsp. sugar
2 tbsp. mirin, or 2 tbsp. dry sherry
2 tsp. rice vinegar
½ tsp. crushed Sichuan peppercorns, or ¼ tsp. crushed black peppercorns

To prepare the sauce, combine the soy sauce, sugar, *mirin* or sherry, vinegar, crushed peppercorns and 3 tablespoons of water in a small bowl. Set aside.

Sprinkle the chicken with the salt and crushed peppercorns. Cut the scallions, cucumber strips and pepper strips to fit inside the breast halves. Arrange some scallions, 2 or 3 cucumber strips, and 2 or 3 pepper strips across the grain of the meat at the wide edge of each cutlet. Roll the chicken around the vegetables

Pour the oil into a deep, heavy-bottomed casserole set over medium-low heat, and stir in the onions. Cover the casserole and cook, stirring occasionally, until the onions are greatly reduced in bulk and quite limp — about 30 minutes.

Uncover the casserole and stir in the flour, black beans and garlic. Cook, stirring, for one minute. Add the wine, 3 cups of the stock, the brandy, potato and some pepper. Lower the chicken into the pot. If necessary, pour in enough additional stock or water to almost cover the bird.

Place a sheet of aluminum foil over the chicken and cover the casserole. Poach gently over medium-low heat, turning the bird several times, until the juices run clear when a thigh is pierced with the tip of a sharp knife — about 45 minutes. Transfer the chicken to a carving board and cover it with the foil to keep it warm.

To prepare the sauce, first skim the fat off the cooking liquid. Set a sieve or colander over a bowl and pour the liquid through it. Reserve ¼ cup of the onions. Transfer the drained potato pieces and the remaining onions to a food processor or blender, add ½ cup of the strained cooking liquid, and purée the mixture until smooth. Pour in an additional cup of the cooking liquid and purée again until smooth.

Pour the sauce into a small pan and warm it over low heat. Remove the sauce from the heat and, if desired, swirl in the butter. (The butter lends richness and gloss to the sauce.)

Carve the chicken into serving pieces. Spoon some sauce over the pieces and scatter the reserved onions over them. Pass the remaining sauce separately.

SUGGESTED ACCOMPANIMENTS: *polenta; green beans.*

Cranberried Chicken

Serves 4
Working time: about 20 minutes
Total time: about 3 hours

Calories **610**
Protein **42g.**
Cholesterol **133mg.**
Total fat **13g.**
Saturated fat **5g.**
Sodium **133mg.**

one 3 lb. chicken, cut into serving pieces and skinned
5 to 7 cups cranberry juice
½ cup loosely packed basil, lightly crushed to bruise the leaves, or 1½ tbsp. dried basil
1 onion, sliced
½ lb. cranberries
½ cup sugar
2 tbsp. raspberry vinegar
1 tsp. cornstarch, mixed with 2 tbsp. water
1 tbsp. unsalted butter, cut into pieces

In a large, nonreactive pot, simmer 5 cups of the cranberry juice with the basil and onion for 10 minutes. Let the liquid cool, then add the chicken pieces. Marinate for two hours at room temperature or overnight in the refrigerator, turning the pieces occasionally.

If needed, pour in enough water to cover the chicken pieces. Bring the liquid to a simmer and reduce the heat. Partially cover the pot. Poach the chicken gently, skimming the foam from the surface, until the juices run clear when a thigh is pierced with the tip of a sharp knife — 15 to 20 minutes.

Simmer the cranberries in 2 cups of juice with the sugar until they almost burst — about seven minutes. Drain the cranberries and discard the liquid.

Transfer the chicken to a heated serving platter and cover it to keep it warm. Strain the poaching liquid and return it to the pot. Add the vinegar and bring the liquid to a boil. Cook over medium-high heat until the

liquid is reduced to about 1½ cups — 15 to 25 minutes. Stir in the cornstarch mixture and the cooked cranberries, and simmer until the sauce has thickened slightly — two or three minutes. Remove the pot from the heat and swirl in the butter. Spoon some of the sauce over the chicken and pass the rest separately.

SUGGESTED ACCOMPANIMENT: *wild rice; braised fennel.*

Chicken Poached in Milk and Curry

Serves 4
Working time: about 15 minutes
Total time: about 1 hour and 15 minutes

Calories **499**
Protein **52g.**
Cholesterol **158mg.**
Total fat **20g.**
Saturated fat **10g.**
Sodium **492mg.**

one 3 lb. chicken, wings removed and reserved for another use, the rest skinned and cut into serving pieces
3 cups milk
2 large onions, thinly sliced (about 3 cups)
4 or 5 bay leaves
2 tsp. fresh thyme, or ½ tsp. dried thyme leaves
3 garlic cloves, crushed
1 tsp. curry powder
½ tsp. salt
freshly ground black pepper
1 cup green peas
1 tbsp. unsalted butter

In a large, heavy-bottomed saucepan over medium heat, combine the milk, onions, bay leaves, thyme, garlic, curry powder, salt and two or three generous grindings of pepper. Bring the liquid just to a simmer, then immediately remove the pan from the heat. Allow the mixture to stand for 30 minutes so that the milk can pick up the flavors; after 15 minutes, preheat the oven to 325° F.

Arrange the chicken pieces in a baking dish just large enough to hold them snugly — no larger than 9 by 13 inches. Bring the milk-and-onion mixture to a simmer again and pour it over the chicken pieces. Set the saucepan aside; do not wash it. Drape the onion slices over any chicken pieces that protrude from the liquid so that the chicken will not dry out during cooking. Put the dish in the oven and poach the chicken until the juices run clear when a thigh is pierced with the tip of a sharp knife — 35 to 40 minutes.

Take the dish from the oven and turn the oven off. Remove the chicken pieces from their poaching liquid

and distribute them among four shallow serving bowls or soup plates. Strain the poaching liquid into the saucepan, and use some of the drained onion slices to garnish each piece of chicken. Discard the remaining onions. Place the bowls in the oven to keep the chicken warm while you finish preparing the sauce.

Cook the liquid in the saucepan over medium heat until it is reduced by about one quarter; there should be approximately 2¼ cups of liquid left. Add the peas and cook them until they are tender — about five minutes. Remove the pan from the heat and whisk in the butter. Pour some of the sauce and peas over the chicken in each bowl and serve immediately.

SUGGESTED ACCOMPANIMENT: *crusty French bread to dunk in the sauce.*

Chicken Fan with Basil-Tomato Sauce

Serves 4
Working time: about 30 minutes
Total time: about 30 minutes

Calories **211**
Protein **29g.**
Cholesterol **73mg.**
Total fat **6g.**
Saturated fat **1g.**
Sodium **90mg.**

4 chicken breast halves, skinned and boned (about 1 lb.)
2 cups unsalted chicken stock
2 cups loosely packed fresh basil leaves (about 4 oz.)
1 garlic clove
2 tsp. mayonnaise
1 tomato, peeled, seeded and chopped

In a pot large enough to hold the chicken breasts snugly, simmer the stock with ½ cup of the basil leaves over medium-low heat for five minutes. Add the breasts to the stock, cover, and poach gently for eight minutes.

Turn the breasts over and poach until they feel firm but springy to the touch — about four minutes more.

Meanwhile, chop the garlic in a food processor or blender. Add the remaining 1½ cups of basil along with ½ cup of water, and purée the mixture. Pour the purée into a sieve and lightly press it with a spoon to remove excess water. To prepare the sauce, scrape the purée into a small bowl and stir in the mayonnaise and half of the chopped tomato.

Lift the chicken breasts from their poaching liquid and pat them dry. Cut each piece diagonally into slices and spread them in a fan pattern on individual serving plates. Spoon about 1½ tablespoons of the sauce at the base of each fan. Scatter the remaining chopped tomato over the top of the sauce.

SUGGESTED ACCOMPANIMENT: *spaghetti squash with Parmesan cheese.*

Braised Chicken Legs with Celery, Shallots and Red Onion

Serves 4
Working time: about 20 minutes
Total time: about 50 minutes

Calories **299**
Protein **28g.**
Cholesterol **98mg.**
Total fat **17g.**
Saturated fat **5g.**
Sodium **346mg.**

4 whole chicken legs, skinned
¼ tsp. salt
freshly ground white pepper
2 tbsp. safflower oil
4 celery stalks, sliced diagonally into ¼-inch-wide slices (about 3 cups)
2 tbsp. shallots, halved lengthwise and thinly sliced
1 cup unsalted chicken stock
½ tsp. celery seeds
1 tbsp. unsalted butter
½ large red onion, thinly sliced
2 tsp. cornstarch, mixed with 1 tbsp. water

Preheat the oven to 350° F. Sprinkle the chicken legs with the salt and pepper. Heat 1 tablespoon of the oil in a large, heavy-bottomed casserole over medium-high heat. Brown the legs in the oil for about two minutes on each side. Transfer the legs to a plate and set them aside.

Add the remaining tablespoon of oil to the casserole and sauté the celery, stirring frequently, for about one minute. Add the shallots and sauté them for another minute, taking care not to brown them. Deglaze the casserole with the stock and stir in the celery seeds. Return the legs to the casserole, bring the liquid to a simmer, and cover. Cook the chicken in the oven until the juices run clear when a thigh is pierced with the tip of a sharp knife — about 25 minutes.

Meanwhile, melt the butter in a heavy-bottomed skillet over medium-low heat, and sauté the onion until translucent — about 10 minutes. Set aside.

Remove the legs from the casserole, strain the liquid into a saucepan, and reserve the celery. To finish the sauce, bring the liquid to a simmer over low heat, stir in the cornstarch mixture, and simmer, stirring constantly, until the sauce thickens — about two minutes. Spread the celery on a warmed serving platter, pour the sauce over the celery and lay the legs on top. Strew the sautéed onions over the chicken and serve at once.

SUGGESTED ACCOMPANIMENT: *puréed carrots and parsnips.*

Spanish-Style Chicken and Saffron Rice

THIS DISH DEPARTS FROM THE TRADITIONAL ARROZ CON POLLO BY CALLING FOR BROWN RICE RATHER THAN WHITE. THE RESULT IS A DEEPER, HEARTIER FLAVOR.

Serves 4
Working time: about 30 minutes
Total time: about 1 hour and 30 minutes

Calories **570**
Protein **41g.**
Cholesterol **103mg.**
Total fat **20g.**
Saturated fat **4g.**
Sodium **409mg.**

one 2½ lb. chicken, skinned and cut into serving pieces
freshly ground black pepper
½ tsp. salt
3 tbsp. virgin olive oil
2 medium onions, thinly sliced
1 cup brown rice
½ cup dry white wine
⅛ tsp. crushed saffron threads
1½ cups unsalted chicken stock
2 tbsp. chopped poblano or other mildly hot chilies
⅛ tsp. crushed cumin seed
2 garlic cloves, finely chopped
2 large ripe tomatoes, peeled, seeded and chopped
1 red and 1 yellow sweet pepper, broiled, skinned, seeded and cut into 1-inch strips
cilantro for garnish (optional)

Sprinkle the chicken pieces with the pepper and ¼ teaspoon of the salt. In a heavy-bottomed 4-quart casserole with a cover, heat 2 tablespoons of the olive oil over medium-high heat. Sauté the chicken until golden brown — about four minutes on each side — and remove to a plate.

Add the remaining tablespoon of oil to the casserole and cook the onions over medium heat until translucent — about 10 minutes. Add the brown rice and cook two minutes, stirring constantly to coat the grains thoroughly; pour in the white wine, bring to a boil, then reduce the heat, cover, and simmer until all the liquid has been absorbed — about eight minutes. Add the saffron to the stock and pour over the rice. Stir in the chilies, cumin seed, the remaining ¼ teaspoon of salt and the garlic. Simmer 15 minutes more and add the tomatoes and chicken, pushing them down into the rice. Cook until the juices run clear when a thigh is pierced with the tip of a sharp knife — about 25 minutes more. Garnish with the pepper strips and cilantro.

the cornstarch mixture and the orange zest, and simmer for five minutes.

Brush the chicken pieces with the glaze and place them under the broiler for a few minutes to brown. Garnish the chicken with the orange segments and pour the sauce over them.

SUGGESTED ACCOMPANIMENT: *braised Belgian endive.*

Saffron Chicken Stew

Serves 4
Working time: about 20 minutes
Total time: about 1 hour and 10 minutes

Calories **594**
Protein **37g.**
Cholesterol **90mg.**
Total fat **17g.**
Saturated fat **3g.**
Sodium **687mg.**

4 chicken legs, skinned, cut into thighs and drumsticks
1 garlic clove, halved
¼ tsp. freshly ground black pepper
½ tsp. salt
2 tbsp. safflower oil
1 medium-size eggplant (about ¾ lb.), cut into 1-inch cubes
1 medium-size yellow summer squash (about ½ lb.), cut into 2-inch cubes
6 scallions
3 celery stalks, trimmed and cut into ½-inch pieces
¼ lb. baby carrots
1 large ripe tomato, peeled, seeded and coarsely chopped
½ tsp. fennel seeds
⅛ tsp. saffron threads, crumbled
1 bay leaf
1 tsp. fresh thyme, or ¼ tsp. dried thyme leaves
1 cup dry vermouth
8 small red potatoes (about 1½ lbs.), with a band peeled from the middle of each
¼ cup coarsely chopped parsley
8 slices French bread, toasted

Rub the chicken pieces with the garlic and reserve it; sprinkle the chicken with the pepper and ¼ teaspoon of the salt. Heat 1 tablespoon of the oil in a 6-quart saucepan over medium heat. Brown the pieces in the oil for about three minutes on each side. Remove the chicken and set it on paper towels to drain.

Add the remaining tablespoon of oil to the pan. Add the garlic, eggplant, squash and the remaining ¼ teaspoon of salt, and sauté lightly over high heat for about one minute. Pour in 1½ quarts of water. Return the chicken pieces to the pan. Add the scallions, celery, carrots, tomato, fennel seeds, saffron, bay leaf, thyme and vermouth, and bring the mixture to a boil. Reduce the heat and simmer gently for about 30 minutes, skimming off the fat from time to time. Add the potatoes and simmer for 15 minutes more. The vegetables should be tender but not soft. Remove the bay leaf and garlic. Add the parsley a few minutes before serving.

Serve the stew in soup bowls, accompanied by the slices of toasted French bread — sprinkled, if you like, with freshly grated Swiss or Parmesan cheese, dusted with paprika and browned under the broiler.

Orange-Glazed Chicken

Serves 4
Working time: about 20 minutes
Total time: about 1 hour

Calories **457**
Protein **40g.**
Cholesterol **124mg.**
Total fat **23g.**
Saturated fat **6g.**
Sodium **421mg.**

one 3 lb. chicken, quartered
½ tsp. salt
freshly ground black pepper
1 tbsp. safflower oil
1 garlic clove, crushed
1 cup unsalted chicken stock
1 tsp. cornstarch, mixed with 1 tbsp. water
1 navel orange, peeled and segmented, the zest grated
Orange glaze
¼ cup orange juice
¼ cup brown sugar
2 tbsp. cider vinegar
1 tsp. Dijon mustard

Sprinkle the chicken with the salt and pepper. Heat the oil in a large, heavy-bottomed skillet over medium-high heat. Add the chicken pieces and brown them lightly — about four minutes on each side. Push the chicken to one side of the skillet, add the garlic, and sauté for 15 seconds. Stir in the stock and allow it to come to a simmer. Redistribute the chicken pieces in the pan. Reduce the heat to low and braise until the juices run clear when a thigh is pierced with the tip of a sharp knife — about 25 minutes.

Meanwhile, make the glaze. In a small saucepan over medium-low heat, combine the orange juice, brown sugar, vinegar and mustard. Bring the mixture to a simmer and cook it for three minutes.

When the chicken is cooked, transfer it to a broiling pan. Skim off and discard the fat from the braising liquid in the skillet. Bring the liquid to a simmer, stir in

Braised Chicken with Plums and Lemons

Serves 4
Working time: about 20 minutes
Total time: about 45 minutes

Calories **261**
Protein **28g.**
Cholesterol **88mg.**
Total fat **11g.**
Saturated fat **5g.**
Sodium **171mg.**

4 chicken breast halves, skinned and boned (about 1 lb.)
2 cups unsalted chicken stock
4 red plums, blanched in the stock for one minute, peeled (skins reserved), cut in half and pits removed
2 tsp. sugar
2 tbsp. unsalted butter
⅛ tsp. salt
freshly ground black pepper
2 tbsp. chopped shallots
8 paper-thin lemon slices

In a saucepan over medium heat, cook the plum skins in the chicken stock until the liquid is reduced to ½ cup. Strain the stock and return it to the pan. Reduce the heat to low, and add the plum halves and sugar. Sim-mer the mixture for one minute, then remove it from the stove and set aside. Preheat the oven to 375° F.

In a heavy-bottomed ovenproof skillet over medium heat, melt the butter. Lay the breasts in the skillet and sauté them lightly on one side for about two minutes. Turn them over, salt and pepper the cooked side, and add the shallots. Place the plum halves cut side down between the breasts. Pour the stock into the skillet and arrange two lemon slices on each breast.

Put the uncovered skillet in the oven. Cook until the chicken feels firm but springy to the touch — about 10 minutes. Remove the skillet from the oven and lift out the plums and breasts with a slotted spoon. Place them on a warmed platter and return the lemon slices to the sauce. Cover the chicken and plums with foil to keep them warm. Simmer the sauce over medium-high heat until it is reduced to about ¼ cup — five to seven min-utes. Put the lemon slices back on top of the breasts and arrange the plums around them. Pour the sauce over all and serve.

SUGGESTED ACCOMPANIMENT: *mashed rutabaga and potatoes.*

Chicken with Orange and Onion

Serves 8
Working time: about 30 minutes
Total time: about 1 hour and 15 minutes

Calories **368**
Protein **42g.**
Cholesterol **125mg.**
Total fat **14g.**
Saturated fat **3g.**
Sodium **257mg.**

two 3 lb. chickens, wings removed, quartered and skinned
2 tbsp. flour
½ tsp. salt
freshly ground black pepper
2 tbsp. safflower oil
zest of 1 orange, julienned
3 onions, thinly sliced
2 tsp. fresh thyme, or ½ tsp. dried thyme leaves
juice of 4 oranges (about 1¾ cup)
2 tbsp. fresh lemon juice
1 tbsp. honey
¾ cup dry white wine

Dust the chicken pieces with the flour. Sprinkle them with ¼ teaspoon of the salt and some of the pepper.

In a large, heavy-bottomed skillet, heat the oil over medium-high heat and sauté the chicken in several batches until golden brown — about five minutes on each side. Transfer the pieces to a 9-by-13-inch baking dish and scatter the orange zest over them.

Preheat the oven to 350° F. Over medium-low heat, cook the onions in the oil in the pan, stirring occasionally, until they are translucent — about 10 minutes. Stir in the thyme and the remaining ¼ teaspoon of salt and spread the mixture over the chicken pieces.

Pour the orange and lemon juice, honey and wine into the skillet. Bring the liquid to a boil and reduce it to about 1 cup. Pour the liquid over the chicken. Cook the pieces uncovered in the oven, basting once with the liquid, until the juices run clear when a thigh is pierced with the tip of a sharp knife — about 35 minutes.

SUGGESTED ACCOMPANIMENTS: *new potatoes cooked in their jackets; steamed celery.*

Braised Chicken with Red and Green Apples

Serves 4
Working time: about 30 minutes
Total time: about 1 hour and 15 minutes

Calories **537**
Protein **40g.**
Cholesterol **137mg.**
Total fat **27g.**
Saturated fat **8g.**
Sodium **561mg.**

one 3 lb. chicken, cut into serving pieces
¼ tsp. freshly ground black pepper
¾ tsp. salt
1 tsp. unsalted butter
1 tbsp. safflower oil
1 small onion, coarsely chopped
1 celery stalk, trimmed and coarsely chopped
½ carrot, coarsely chopped
1 garlic clove, crushed
1½ tart green apples, peeled, quartered and thinly sliced
1 tbsp. chopped fresh tarragon, or 1 tsp. dried tarragon, with some whole leaves reserved for a garnish if fresh tarragon is used
1 cup dry vermouth
1 cup unsalted chicken stock
2 tsp. plain low-fat yogurt
2 tbsp. heavy cream

Apple garnish

1 tbsp. sugar
1 tsp. tarragon vinegar
3 tbsp. unsalted chicken stock
½ unpeeled firm red apple and ½ unpeeled tart green apple, quartered and cut into ¼-inch slices

Sprinkle the chicken pieces with the pepper and ½ teaspoon of the salt. Melt the butter with the oil in a large, heavy-bottomed sauté pan over medium-high heat and sauté the pieces on both sides until golden — about four minutes on each side. Put the pieces on paper towels to drain.

Pour off all but 1 tablespoon of the fat. Add the onion, celery, carrot, garlic, apples and tarragon, and cook, stirring occasionally, until the onions are translucent — about five minutes.

Add the vermouth and reduce the liquid by two thirds. Return the chicken to the pan, add the stock, and bring the liquid to a boil. Reduce the heat, cover tightly, and simmer until the juices run clear when a thigh is pierced with the tip of a sharp knife — about 20 minutes. With a slotted spoon, transfer the contents of the pan to a heated serving platter and keep warm.

To make a sauce, pour 1½ cups of the braising liquid into a small saucepan. Skim off the fat, then bring the liquid to a simmer and reduce it by half. Add the remaining ¼ teaspoon of salt, the yogurt and the cream. Whisk until well blended.

To prepare the apple garnish, melt the sugar in a heavy-bottomed saucepan over low heat, stirring with a wooden spoon until the sugar caramelizes — it will turn a honey brown. Standing back from the stove to avoid being splattered, add the vinegar and the stock all at once; the caramelized sugar will solidify. Continue cooking until the sugar melts once more and the liquid becomes syrupy. Add the apple slices and toss them in the liquid for about one minute. Arrange them around and on top of the chicken and sprinkle with the fresh tarragon leaves. Pass the sauce separately.

SUGGESTED ACCOMPANIMENT: *braised leeks or stewed onions.*

Chicken Braised with White Beans and Tomatoes

THIS IS A LOW-FAT VARIATION ON THE CASSOULET OF SOUTHWESTERN FRANCE.

Serves 6
Working time: about 1 hour
Total time: about 1 day

Calories **506**
Protein **42g.**
Cholesterol **98mg.**
Total fat **19g.**
Saturated fat **4g.**
Sodium **520mg.**

one 3½ lb. chicken, skin and wing tips removed, cut into serving pieces
1 lb. dried navy beans, soaked overnight in water and drained
½ tsp. salt
freshly ground black pepper
1 tbsp. fresh thyme, or ¾ tsp. dried thyme leaves
2 tbsp. safflower oil
½ cup dry white wine
2 leeks, trimmed, halved lengthwise and cut into ½-inch pieces
one 16 oz. can whole tomatoes, the tomatoes halved and the liquid reserved
1 tbsp. fresh rosemary, or ¾ tsp. dried rosemary
6 garlic cloves, finely chopped
3 bay leaves
2½ cups unsalted chicken stock
1 cup dry bread crumbs
2 tbsp. virgin olive oil
2 tsp. chopped fresh parsley

Place the beans in a large saucepan or casserole and cover them with 2 inches of water. Add ¼ teaspoon of the salt and bring to a boil over high heat. Boil the beans for 10 minutes, skimming off foam as it accumulates. Reduce the heat to low. Gently stir in the pepper and one third of the thyme. Cover the pan and simmer for 35 minutes. Drain the beans. Preheat the oven to 375° F.

In a large, heavy-bottomed skillet, heat the safflower oil over medium-high heat. Add the chicken pieces and brown them lightly — about three minutes on each side. With a slotted spoon, transfer the chicken pieces to a plate. Pour off any accumulated fat from the skillet and reserve it. Pour the wine into the skillet and deglaze the pan over medium-high heat, scraping up any brown bits with a wooden spoon.

When the wine boils, add the leeks, the tomatoes and their liquid, the rosemary, the remaining two thirds of the thyme, the remaining ¼ teaspoon of salt, and half of the garlic. Reduce the heat to low and simmer the mixture, stirring frequently, until the vegetables are tender — about 10 minutes. Then remove the skillet from the heat.

Spread the remaining garlic evenly over the bottom of a large, deep casserole. Add half of the cooked beans in an even layer, then distribute the chicken pieces on the beans and top with the bay leaves. Spoon half of the tomato-and-leek mixture over the chicken, then add the remaining beans in another even layer, and spoon the remaining tomato-and-leek mixture over them. Pour in 1½ cups of the stock and sprinkle the bread crumbs over all. Dribble the reserved fat and the olive oil onto the bread crumbs.

Bake the casserole for 45 minutes. Carefully pour in the remaining cup of stock around the edges of the dish so as not to soak the bread-crumb topping. Bake for about 30 minutes more, or until a golden brown crust has formed and the beans are tender.

Scatter the parsley over the top and serve.

SUGGESTED ACCOMPANIMENT: *romaine lettuce salad.*
EDITOR'S NOTE: *This dish can be prepared a day in advance and refrigerated overnight, further melding the flavors. Before serving, warm the dish in a 350° F. oven for 35 minutes.*

Jellied Chicken
with Lemon and Dill

Serves 8
Working time: about 30 minutes
Total time: about 1 day

Calories **339**
Protein **43g.**
Cholesterol **125mg.**
Total fat **14g.**
Saturated fat **3g.**
Sodium **236mg.**

two 3 lb. chickens, skinned and cut into serving pieces
¼ tsp. salt
freshly ground black pepper
2 tbsp. virgin olive oil
1 large onion, finely chopped
⅓ cup chopped fresh dill
4 cups unsalted chicken stock
3 large carrots, thinly sliced
¾ cup green peas
⅓ cup fresh lemon juice

Sprinkle the chicken pieces with the salt and pepper. Heat the olive oil in a large, heavy-bottomed skillet and sauté as many pieces as will fit without crowding over medium-high heat until golden — about five minutes on each side. Arrange the pieces in a large casserole.

In the remaining oil, cook the onion over medium-low heat until translucent — about 10 minutes; stir in half of the dill. Spoon the onion mixture onto the chicken pieces. Pour the stock over all and bring to a simmer on top of the stove. After 20 minutes, turn the pieces, add the carrots and peas, and continue cooking until the juices run clear when a thigh is pierced with the tip of a sharp knife — about 10 minutes more.

Pour the lemon juice over the chicken and vegetables, and cool to room temperature. Sprinkle the remaining dill on top. Refrigerate for six hours or overnight to allow the natural gelatin to set. Serve cold.

SUGGESTED ACCOMPANIMENTS: *rice salad; sliced tomatoes.*

EDITOR'S NOTE: *If fresh dill is unavailable, parsley, tarragon or chervil may be substituted.*

Chicken Mole

THIS IS A VARIATION ON MOLE POBLANO, HERE MADE WITH
CHICKEN RATHER THAN TURKEY

Serves 6
Working time: about 1 hour
Total time: about 2 hours

Calories **294**
Protein **28g.**
Cholesterol **98mg.**
Total fat **17g.**
Saturated fat **4g.**
Sodium **242mg.**

12 chicken thighs, skinned and boned
1 tsp. coriander seeds
¼ tsp. anise seeds
2 garlic cloves, coarsely chopped
¼ tsp. cinnamon
¼ tsp. salt
¼ tsp. freshly ground black pepper
2 tbsp. safflower oil
2 jalapeño peppers or other hot chili peppers, halved lengthwise, seeded, and finely chopped (see caution, page 25)
1 onion, chopped
2 small ripe tomatoes, peeled, seeded and chopped
1¼ cups unsalted chicken stock
½ oz. unsweetened chocolate, grated
2 tsp. cornstarch, mixed with 2 tbsp. red wine

In a small, heavy-bottomed saucepan, toast the coriander and anise seeds over medium heat for three to four minutes, shaking the pan frequently. Put the seeds along with the garlic, cinnamon, salt and pepper in a mortar; using a pestle, grind the seasonings to a paste.

Heat 1 tablespoon of the oil in a large, heavy-bottomed skillet over medium heat. Sauté the chilies in the oil, stirring constantly until they begin to brown — about three minutes. Then add the onion, tomatoes and seasoning paste. Cook until almost all the liquid evaporates — about 10 minutes. Transfer the mixture to a bowl and set aside.

Clean the pan and set it over medium-high heat. Add the remaining tablespoon of oil. Sauté the chicken thighs, in two batches if necessary, so that the pieces do not touch, until they are brown — about four minutes on each side. Pour off the fat. Add the stock, onion-and-tomato mixture, and chocolate. Bring the sauce to a boil and stir well to melt the chocolate. Reduce the heat to low, cover, and simmer until the juices run clear when a thigh is pierced with the tip of a sharp knife — about 20 minutes.

Transfer the pieces to a serving platter and keep them warm. Stir the cornstarch-and-wine mixture into the sauce and simmer, stirring frequently, until the sauce is reduced to approximately 1½ cups — about seven minutes. Pour the sauce over the chicken.

SUGGESTED ACCOMPANIMENTS: *yellow rice; black beans; orange and onion salad.*

Curried Chicken with Chutney and Raisins

Serves 4
Working time: about 30 minutes
Total time: about 1 hour

Calories **476**
Protein **45g.**
Cholesterol **126mg.**
Total fat **22g.**
Saturated fat **4g.**
Sodium **437mg.**

| one 3 lb. chicken, skinned and cut into serving pieces |
| ½ tsp. salt |
| ½ tsp. freshly ground black pepper |
| ¼ cup cornmeal |
| 3 tbsp. safflower oil |
| 1 onion, finely chopped |
| 1 carrot, finely chopped |
| ½ small green pepper, finely chopped |
| 3 garlic cloves, finely chopped |
| ¾ lb. tomatoes, preferably the Italian plum variety, peeled, seeded and coarsely chopped, with juice reserved |
| 1 ½ cups unsalted chicken stock |

| 1 tbsp. curry powder |
| 2 tsp. mango chutney |
| 1 bay leaf |
| 1 ½ tbsp. dark raisins |
| 1 ½ tbsp. golden raisins |
| 1 tbsp. sesame seeds |

Sprinkle the chicken pieces with the salt and pepper, and dredge them lightly in the cornmeal. In a heavy-bottomed casserole large enough to hold the chicken in a single layer, heat 2 tablespoons of the oil over medium heat. Brown the chicken for two minutes on each side. Remove the chicken and set it aside. Preheat the oven to 350° F.

Put the remaining tablespoon of oil into the casserole. Add the onion, carrot and green pepper, and sauté lightly for about one minute. Add the garlic and sauté for 30 seconds more. Pour in the tomatoes, their reserved juice and the stock. Stir in the curry powder,

chutney, bay leaf, and 1 tablespoon of each type of raisin. Return the chicken to the casserole and bring the liquid to a simmer. Bake the casserole, covered, for 10 minutes. While it is baking, brown the sesame seeds in a piepan in the oven — about 10 minutes.

When the breasts feel firm but springy to the touch, remove them from the oven and set them aside on a plate, leaving the other chicken pieces in the casserole. Cover the breasts with aluminum foil to keep them warm. Bake the other pieces until the juices run clear when a thigh is pierced with the tip of a sharp knife — about five minutes more. Serve the chicken straight from the casserole or arranged on a platter, with the toasted sesame seeds and the remaining raisins scattered across the top.

SUGGESTED ACCOMPANIMENTS: *steamed rice; side dishes of yogurt, unsalted peanuts and chopped banana.*

Chicken Legs with Dark Rum, Papaya, Mango and Banana

Serves 4
Working time: about 30 minutes
Total time: about 50 minutes

Calories **538**
Protein **30g.**
Cholesterol **112mg.**
Total fat **18g.**
Saturated fat **6g.**
Sodium **397mg.**

4 whole chicken legs, skinned, cut into thighs and drumsticks
½ tsp. salt
freshly ground white pepper
1 tbsp. safflower oil
1 large onion, cut into eighths, layers separated
2 garlic cloves, finely chopped
2 tsp. finely chopped fresh ginger
1 cup dark rum
2 cups unsalted chicken stock
¼ cup heavy cream
1 large tomato, peeled, cored, seeded and cut into large chunks
1 medium papaya, scooped into balls with a melon-baller or cut into cubes, with the extra flesh chopped and reserved
1 small mango, peeled and cut into cubes
1 small banana, cut into ½-inch slices
⅛ tsp. freshly grated nutmeg

Sprinkle the chicken with ¼ teaspoon of the salt and some pepper. In a large, heavy-bottomed casserole, heat the oil over medium heat. Brown the chicken pieces lightly — about four minutes on each side.

Add the onion and cook it with the chicken, stirring frequently, until the onion is translucent — about five minutes. Add the garlic and ginger, and cook for one minute more. Remove the casserole from the heat and allow it to cool for one minute. Reserve 1 teaspoon of the rum and set it aside, and pour the rest into the casserole. Return the casserole to the heat and simmer until the liquid is reduced by half — about five minutes.

Add the stock to the casserole and bring it to a boil. Reduce the heat to low, and simmer until the juices run clear when a thigh is pierced with a sharp knife — about five minutes more. Transfer the chicken pieces to a heated serving platter and cover them with foil.

In a saucepan, bring the cream, tomato and extra papaya flesh to a simmer. Pour in the braising liquid from the casserole and simmer until the sauce thickens slightly — about three minutes. Purée the mixture in a food processor or blender, and return it to the pan.

Add the papaya balls or cubes, mango, banana, nutmeg, the reserved teaspoon of rum and the remaining ¼ teaspoon of salt, and cook just until the fruit is heated through — about one minute. Remove the foil from the chicken and pour the sauce over the pieces. Serve immediately.

SUGGESTED ACCOMPANIMENT: *yellow rice.*

heat to medium high, stirring until the excess liquid evaporates — about seven minutes. Pour in the wine and the reserved tomato juice. Simmer until the liquid is reduced by one third — about 10 minutes. Return the drumsticks to the pan, immersing them in the sauce. Season with the remaining ⅛ teaspoon of salt and some additional pepper.

Cover the skillet and braise the chicken in the oven until the meat is tender and clings loosely to the bone — about 30 minutes. Arrange it on a deep platter.

Place the uncovered skillet over high heat. Add the parsley, then further reduce the sauce by one third — about five minutes. Spoon this thickened sauce over the drumsticks and serve.

SUGGESTED ACCOMPANIMENT: *pasta tossed with the extra cacciatore sauce.*

Chicken Drumsticks Cacciatore

Serves 6
Working time: about 40 minutes
Total time: about 1 hour and 30 minutes

Calories **307**	12 chicken drumsticks
Protein **30g.**	¼ tsp. salt
Cholesterol **96mg.**	freshly ground black pepper
Total fat **14g.**	1 tbsp. virgin olive oil
Saturated fat **3g.**	1 onion, finely chopped (about ¾ cup)
Sodium **365mg.**	1 small carrot, cut into ⅛-inch slices
	1 small celery stalk, cut into ⅛-inch slices
	1 large green pepper, seeded, deribbed and cut into ½-inch squares
	1 small red pepper, seeded, deribbed and cut into ½-inch squares
	5 garlic cloves, finely chopped
	2 tsp. fresh oregano leaves, chopped, or ¾ tsp. dried oregano
	1 tsp. fresh thyme, or ¼ tsp. dried thyme leaves
	one 28-oz. can plum tomatoes, drained and chopped, with the juice reserved
	½ cup dry white wine
	2 tbsp. chopped parsley

Rub the chicken with ⅛ teaspoon of the salt and the pepper. In a heavy-bottomed ovenproof skillet with a lid, heat the oil over medium-high heat. Add the drumsticks and brown them on all sides — about 12 minutes. Transfer the pieces to a plate.

Reduce the heat to medium. Combine the onion, carrot, celery, green and red peppers, and garlic in the skillet. Sprinkle the oregano and thyme over the vegetables and stir. Sauté until the peppers are softened — about five minutes. Preheat the oven to 325° F.

Add the chopped tomato to the skillet and raise the

Chicken Breasts with Yellow Squash in Red Wine Sauce

Serves 4
Working time: about 35 minutes
Total time: about 50 minutes

Calories **383**	4 chicken breast halves, skinned and boned (about 1 lb.)
Protein **29g.**	¼ tsp. salt
Cholesterol **86mg.**	½ tsp. freshly ground black pepper
Total fat **16g.**	2 medium yellow summer squashes, sliced into ½-inch-thick rounds
Saturated fat **5g.**	2 tbsp. safflower oil
Sodium **250mg.**	1 garlic clove, finely chopped
	1½ cups unsalted chicken stock
	1 tbsp. finely chopped shallots
	½ cup finely chopped onions
	¼ cup finely chopped celery
	¼ cup finely chopped carrots
	2 cups red wine
	1 tbsp. heavy cream
	½ tsp. finely chopped fresh sage, or ¼ tsp. dried sage
	1 tbsp. unsalted butter

Sprinkle the chicken breasts with ⅛ teaspoon of the salt and ¼ teaspoon of the pepper. Sprinkle the squash with the remaining salt and pepper. Heat 1 tablespoon of the oil in a heavy-bottomed skillet over medium-high heat. Lightly brown the breasts in the skillet — about two minutes on each side. Remove the breasts and sauté the squash and garlic for about one minute in the oil remaining in the skillet. Remove the squash and deglaze the pan with ½ cup of the stock. Reduce the heat to low and return the breasts to the skillet. Simmer, partly covered, until the meat feels firm but springy to the touch — 10 to 12 minutes.

While the breasts are cooking, prepare the sauce.

Heat the remaining tablespoon of oil over medium-low heat in a heavy-bottomed saucepan. Add the shallots, onions, celery and carrots, and cook until the onions are translucent — about 10 minutes. Pour in the wine, increase the heat to medium, and cook until reduced by half — about seven minutes. Add the cream, sage and the remaining cup of stock. Again reduce by half. Purée the sauce in a food processor or blender and

strain it. When the chicken breasts are done, move them to the side of the skillet and pour in the sauce. Stir the sauce to mix it thoroughly, then whisk in the butter. Return the squash to the skillet to heat it through, and serve.

SUGGESTED ACCOMPANIMENT: *sautéed green peppers and onions.*

Chicken Legs Stewed with Prunes

Serves 4
Working time: about 40 minutes
Total time: about 3 hours and 45 minutes

Calories **500**
Protein **30g.**
Cholesterol **98mg.**
Total fat **12g.**
Saturated fat **4g.**
Sodium **263mg.**

4 large chicken legs, skinned
1 cup brandy
20 pitted prunes (about ⅓ lb.)
1 tbsp. unsalted butter
¼ tsp. salt
freshly ground black pepper
1 large onion, cut in half and thinly sliced
1 large carrot, cut diagonally into ¼-inch slices
4 garlic cloves, finely chopped
1 tsp. dry mustard
1 tsp. fresh thyme, or ¼ tsp. dried thyme leaves
1¾ cup unsalted chicken stock
10 parsley stems, tied in a bunch with butcher's twine
3 tbsp. fresh lemon juice
1 tbsp. chopped fresh parsley

Pour the brandy over the prunes and marinate them for at least two hours at room temperature or overnight in the refrigerator.

Heat the butter in a large, heavy-bottomed skillet over medium-high heat. Lightly brown the chicken legs for about five minutes on each side. Sprinkle the salt and pepper over the legs and transfer them to a large, heavy-bottomed casserole, and set them aside. In the skillet used to brown the legs, combine the onion, carrot, garlic, mustard and thyme, and reduce the heat to medium. Sauté, stirring frequently, until the onion is translucent — five to seven minutes.

Preheat the oven to 325° F.

Add the prunes, brandy and stock to the onion-and-carrot mixture. Let the liquid come to a simmer and continue cooking for three minutes, then empty the skillet into the casserole; the mixture should nearly cover the legs. Drop in the bunch of parsley stems.

Cover the casserole and cook in the oven for one hour. Reduce the oven temperature to 200° F. Transfer the legs to a serving platter and cover them with foil. Open the oven door to partially vent the heat, and put the platter inside. Add the lemon juice to the sauce, remove the bunch of parsley and reduce the liquid by half over medium heat — 15 to 20 minutes. Pour the sauce over the chicken legs and serve immediately, garnished with the chopped parsley.

SUGGESTED ACCOMPANIMENT: *steamed cauliflower.*

Lemon-Mustard Chicken with Root Vegetables

Serves 6
Working time: about 20 minutes
Total time: about 45 minutes

Calories **263**
Protein **29g.**
Cholesterol **80mg.**
Total fat **9g.**
Saturated fat **3g.**
Sodium **261mg.**

6 large chicken breast halves, skinned, fat removed
1 tbsp. safflower oil
2 tbsp. unsalted butter
1 onion, cut into 12 pieces
1 garlic clove, finely chopped
½ cup dry sherry
¼ tsp. salt
freshly ground black pepper
2 tbsp. fresh lemon juice
2 tbsp. Dijon mustard
2 cups unsalted chicken stock
2 carrots, cut into ½-inch rounds
2 parsnips, cut into ½-inch rounds
1 small rutabaga, or 2 medium white turnips, peeled and cut into ½-inch cubes
zest of 1 lemon, grated
¼ cup chopped parsley

Heat the oil and butter in a large, heavy-bottomed skillet or casserole over medium-high heat. Sauté the chicken, bone side up, until the pieces turn golden — about four minutes. Remove the chicken and set it aside. Add the onion pieces to the pan, and sauté for two minutes. Add the garlic and sauté for about 15 seconds. Pour off the fat. Add the sherry to deglaze the pan, and stir. Lower the heat and simmer until the liquid is reduced by half — about four minutes.

Return the chicken breasts, bone side down, to the simmering mixture and sprinkle them with the salt and pepper. Stir in the lemon juice, mustard and stock; then add the carrots, parsnips and rutabaga or turnips. Bring the sauce to a boil, stirring. Reduce the heat to low, partially cover the pan, and simmer until the vegetables are tender — about 20 minutes. Arrange the chicken and vegetables in a serving dish. Pour the sauce over the chicken, and garnish with the lemon zest and parsley before serving.

SUGGESTED ACCOMPANIMENTS: *curly endive salad; pumpernickel bread.*

Braised Chicken, Almonds and Chick-Peas

IN THE MOROCCAN ORIGINAL, THE SKIN IS LEFT
ON. IN THIS SKINLESS VERSION, WHOLE-WHEAT FLOUR
ADDS COLOR AND FLAVOR TO THE CHICKEN.

Serves 4
Working time: about 20 minutes
Total time: about 1 day

Calories **681**
Protein **51g.**
Cholesterol **105mg.**
Total fat **25g.**
Saturated fat **4g.**
Sodium **617mg.**

one 2½ lb. chicken, skinned and cut into quarters
1 cup dried chick-peas, soaked overnight in water and drained
½ cup whole toasted almonds, coarsely chopped
1 tsp. whole-wheat flour
¼ tsp. salt
¼ tsp. freshly ground black pepper
2 tbsp. virgin olive oil
1 large onion, chopped
4 garlic cloves, finely chopped
½ tsp. powdered ginger
⅛ tsp. turmeric
⅛ tsp. cinnamon
⅛ tsp. ground cumin
2 tbsp. dried currants
2½ cups unsalted chicken stock
2 tbsp. fresh lemon juice
1⅔ cups precooked couscous

Put the soaked chick-peas in a large saucepan, covering with cold water to a level 1 inch above them. Bring to a boil, then lower the heat and simmer for 60 minutes. Drain the chick-peas and place them in an oven-proof casserole with the almonds.

Preheat the oven to 350° F. Mix the flour with the salt and pepper, and dust the chicken pieces all over.

Sauté them in the olive oil in a large heavy-bottomed skillet over medium-high heat until they are nicely browned — about five minutes on each side. Remove the pieces and arrange them on top of the chick-peas and almonds.

In the same skillet, cook the onion over medium-low heat until translucent — about 10 minutes. Add the garlic, ginger, turmeric, cinnamon, cumin and currants, and mix well. Cook another two to three minutes. Spoon the mixture onto the chicken.

Add 1 cup of the stock and the lemon juice and bring to a simmer on top of the stove, then cover the casserole and place it in the oven. Cook until the chicken juices run clear when a thigh is pierced with the tip of a sharp knife — about 45 minutes.

Shortly before the chicken is done, bring the remaining 1½ cups of chicken stock to a boil in a saucepan and slowly pour in the couscous, stirring continuously. Remove from the heat and allow to stand five minutes, then fluff with a fork.

Spoon the couscous onto a serving platter and arrange the chicken pieces, chick-peas and almonds on top. Pour the juices over all.

SUGGESTED ACCOMPANIMENTS: *yogurt; steamed Swiss chard.*

Chicken Casserole with Dried Fruits and Caramelized Onions

Serves 4
Working time: about 30 minutes
Total time: about 1 hour and 45 minutes

Calories **587**
Protein **34g.**
Cholesterol **108mg.**
Total fat **20g.**
Saturated fat **6g.**
Sodium **468mg.**

8 chicken thighs, skinned
1 tbsp. safflower oil
1 tbsp. plus ½ tsp. unsalted butter
½ tsp. salt
freshly ground black pepper
1 cup brown rice
1 small onion, chopped
2½ cups unsalted chicken stock
1 bouquet garni, made by tying together 2 sprigs fresh thyme, several parsley stems and 1 bay leaf (if fresh thyme is unavailable, tie up ½ tsp. of dried thyme leaves in a piece of cheesecloth with the other herbs)
⅓ cup dried apricots, cut in half
¼ cup golden raisins
¼ cup dried currants
1 tbsp. grainy mustard
¼ tsp. grated orange zest (optional)
1 cup pearl onions, blanched for 30 seconds and peeled, or 1 cup frozen pearl onions without sauce
⅛ tsp. sugar

In a 4-quart heavy-bottomed casserole, heat the oil and the tablespoon of the butter over medium-high heat. Cook four of the chicken thighs on one side until lightly browned — about four minutes. Turn the thighs and sprinkle them with ⅛ teaspoon of the salt and some pepper. Sauté them on the second side for three minutes more. Remove the thighs from the casserole and set them aside. Repeat the process with the remaining thighs and set them aside.

Reduce the heat to medium. Add the rice and chopped onion to the casserole and cook until the grains of rice are translucent — about five minutes. Add 1½ cups of the stock, the remaining ¼ teaspoon of salt and the bouquet garni. Bring the liquid to a boil. Lower the heat, cover the pot, and simmer for 20 minutes. Preheat the oven to 350° F.

Stir the apricots, raisins, currants, mustard and orange zest, if using, into the casserole. Return the chick-

en pieces to the casserole, pressing them down into the rice. Pour the remaining cup of stock over the top. Cover and bake in the oven for 35 minutes.

Meanwhile, to caramelize the pearl onions, put them in a small skillet with the sugar and the ½ teaspoon of butter. Pour in just enough water to cover the onions. Boil rapidly until no water remains — 10 to 15 minutes. Watching the onions carefully lest they burn, shake the pan until they are evenly browned all over.

Add the caramelized onions to the casserole and bake until the rice is tender — about 15 minutes more. Remove the bouquet garni and serve the chicken from the casserole accompanied by the rice, fruit and onion.

SUGGESTED ACCOMPANIMENT: *Belgian endive salad.*

Chicken Fricassee with Watercress

Serves 4
Working time: about 45 minutes
Total time: about 45 minutes

Calories **249**
Protein **18g.**
Cholesterol **61mg.**
Total fat **10g.**
Saturated fat **4g.**
Sodium **249mg.**

4 large chicken thighs, skinned, boned, excess fat removed, the meat cut into 1-inch cubes
½ cup plain low-fat yogurt
2 tbsp. light cream
2 tbsp. cornstarch, mixed with ¼ cup water
2 tsp. fresh thyme, or ½ tsp. dried thyme leaves
1 tsp. fresh rosemary, or ¼ tsp. dried rosemary
1 tbsp. unsalted butter
2 carrots, julienned
½ lb. mushrooms, thickly sliced (about 3 cups)
3 tbsp. finely chopped shallots
½ cup dry white wine
½ cup unsalted chicken stock
4 garlic cloves, finely chopped
¼ tsp. salt
2 bunches watercress, thick stems removed

In a small bowl, combine the yogurt, cream, cornstarch mixture, thyme and rosemary. Set aside.

Melt the butter over medium heat in a large, heavy-bottomed skillet. Add the carrots and cook for two minutes, stirring once. Stir in the chicken, mushrooms, shallots, wine, stock, garlic, salt and the yogurt mixture. Reduce the heat to medium low, cover, and cook for five minutes.

Uncover the pan and stir well. Scatter the watercress over the top but do not stir it in; the watercress should be allowed to steam. Cover again and cook until the chicken pieces are done — about five minutes more. Drain the contents of the skillet in a large colander or sieve, catching the sauce in a bowl. Put the contents of the colander on a platter and set aside to keep warm.

Return the sauce to the skillet. Over medium heat, whisking occasionally to keep the sauce from burning, reduce it by half, to approximately 1¼ cups. This should take 10 to 15 minutes.

Return the chicken mixture to the skillet, and stir to coat the chicken with the sauce. Serve at once.

SUGGESTED ACCOMPANIMENT: *pasta with tomato and Parmesan cheese.*

Braised Chicken with Potatoes, Leeks and Kale

Serves 4
Working time: about 30 minutes
Total time: about 1 hour and 15 minutes

Calories **439**	
Protein **42g.**	one 3½ lb. chicken
Cholesterol **123mg**	freshly ground black pepper
Total fat **23g.**	¾ tsp. salt
Saturated fat **6g.**	1 tbsp. safflower oil
Sodium **539mg.**	1 leek, halved lengthwise, cleaned thoroughly, and cut into ½-inch-thick slices
	2 tbsp. thinly sliced shallots
	¼ lb. fresh kale, stemmed, washed and coarsely chopped
	2 tbsp. fresh thyme, or ½ tsp. dried thyme leaves
	½ tsp. cayenne pepper
	3 red potatoes, unpeeled, cut into 1½-inch pieces

Rub the inside of the chicken with pepper and ¼ teaspoon of the salt, and truss the bird.

In a large, heavy-bottomed casserole, heat the oil over medium-high heat. Add the leek, shallots and kale, and sauté until the kale begins to wilt. Pour in four cups of water, then add the remaining salt, some more pepper and the thyme. Place the chicken in the casserole and sprinkle the cayenne pepper over it. Bring the liquid to a boil, reduce the heat to low, partially cover the casserole, and simmer for 50 minutes.

With a large fork, lift the chicken from the casserole and place it on a warmed platter. Cover it with foil to keep it warm. Skim off any fat in the casserole. Add the potatoes and simmer until they are tender — about 10 minutes. Arrange the vegetables around the chicken and pour the braising liquid over it.

Chicken Rolled in Grape Leaves

Serves 4
Working time: about 30 minutes
Total time: about 1 day

Calories **464**	¾ lb. chicken breast meat, cut into ½-inch cubes
Protein **36g.**	2 cups unsalted chicken stock
Cholesterol **62mg.**	
Total fat **19g.**	1 cup yellow split peas, soaked overnight and drained
Saturated fat **4g.**	1 tsp. fresh mint, chopped
Sodium **550mg.**	2 tbsp. cilantro, chopped
	¾ tsp. salt
	freshly ground black pepper
	1 medium eggplant, peeled and cut into ½-inch cubes
	2 tbsp. safflower oil
	5 garlic cloves, peeled and crushed lightly so that they remain whole
	2 tbsp. sesame paste
	4 black olives, pitted
	2 tsp. fresh lemon juice
	8 grape leaves
	4 large cherry tomatoes, halved
	1 tbsp. unsalted butter, melted

Put the stock, peas, mint, 1 tablespoon of the cilantro, ¼ teaspoon of the salt and some pepper in a saucepan and bring to a boil. Reduce the heat, cover, and simmer until the peas are cooked — about 45 minutes.

Meanwhile, toss the eggplant cubes with an additional ¼ teaspoon of the salt and place them on paper towels to drain.

Season the chicken cubes with the remaining ¼ teaspoon of salt and some pepper. Heat 1 tablespoon of the oil in a heavy-bottomed skillet over medium-high heat. Sauté the chicken cubes until lightly browned — about four minutes. Transfer to a mixing bowl.

Add the remaining tablespoon of oil to the skillet and sauté the garlic cloves for two minutes. Transfer them to a food processor or blender. Sauté the eggplant cubes in the oil remaining in the pan until they brown — about five minutes. Add the eggplant, sesame paste, the remaining tablespoon of cilantro, the olives, lemon juice and some black pepper to the food processor or blender, and purée. Reserve 2 tablespoons of the mixture for the tomato garnish and mix the remaining purée with the chicken to make a filling. Preheat the oven to 350° F.

Rinse the grape leaves and lay them flat. Place 2 tablespoons of the filling on each leaf. Fold the sides of a leaf in to encase the filling, and roll it up. Repeat with the remaining leaves. Spread the cooked split peas in the bottom of a baking dish and place the rolled grape leaves on top. Top each tomato half with a dab of the reserved eggplant mixture and arrange the tomatoes around the sides of the dish. Bake for 15 minutes. Brush the grape leaves with the melted butter just before serving.

Plum-Coated Chicken with Nappa Cabbage

Serves 8
Working time: about 1 hour and 30 minutes
Total time: about 2 hours

Calories **268**
Protein **23g.**
Cholesterol **71mg.**
Total fat **13g.**
Saturated fat **4g.**
Sodium **317mg.**

two 3 lb. chickens, skinned and cut into serving pieces, the wings reserved for later use
2 small heads Nappa (Chinese) cabbage, about 1½ lb. each
4 cups unsalted chicken stock
5 large ripe red plums
2 tbsp. honey
½ cup red wine vinegar
2 tbsp. unsalted butter
2 tbsp. fresh lemon juice
1 tbsp. safflower oil
¾ tsp. salt
1 tbsp. virgin olive oil

Discard the brown outer leaves of the cabbage. Cut 2 inches off the base of each cabbage; rinse the leaves and pat them dry. Cut out and discard the white core at the base of each leaf. Slice the leaves into 2-inch squares and set them aside.

Bring the stock to a boil in a saucepan. Cut a shallow cross on the bottom of each plum, and boil the plums in the stock until the skin begins to peel away from the cross — about two minutes. Peel the plums over the stock, letting their skins and juice fall into the hot liquid, and set the plums aside. Stir 1 tablespoon of the honey and ¼ cup of the vinegar into the stock. Reduce the liquid over medium-high heat to 2 cups — about 15 minutes — and set it aside.

Meanwhile, prepare the plum sauce. Cut the plums in half, remove their pits and cut the halves into cubes. Melt the butter in a large, heavy-bottomed saucepan over medium heat. Add the plums and the remaining tablespoon of honey and the remaining ¼ cup of vinegar. Cook, stirring often, until the plums are reduced to a dense, pasty consistency — 45 to 60 minutes. Stir in ½ cup of the stock and the lemon juice. Transfer the plum sauce to a food processor or blender. Process until smooth — about 30 seconds — stopping once to scrape down the sides.

Simmer the remaining stock to reduce it to ¾ cup — 10 to 15 minutes. Strain it and set it aside.

While the stock is simmering, heat the safflower oil in a large, heavy-bottomed skillet over medium-high heat. Sauté half of the chicken pieces on one side until brown — about four minutes. Turn the pieces, sprinkle them with ¼ teaspoon of the salt, and cook on the second side until brown — three to four minutes more. Transfer the pieces to a platter. Repeat the procedure with the remaining chicken pieces. Reserve the skillet for the cabbage. Preheat the oven to 400° F.

Arrange the chicken pieces, smooth side up, in a large ovenproof serving dish. Brush a thick coat of plum sauce over each piece. Whisk the remaining sauce into the reduced stock. Bake the chicken until the juices run clear when a thigh is pierced with the tip of a sharp knife — about 30 minutes.

While the chicken is baking, cook the cabbage. Cover the bottom of a large pot with 1 inch of water, lower a vegetable steamer into the pot and bring the water to a boil. Add the cabbage squares, cover tightly, and steam until the leaves are wilted, stirring once — about six minutes. Drain the cabbage well.

Heat the olive oil in the skillet over medium heat. Add the cabbage and sprinkle it with the remaining ¼ teaspoon of salt. Toss well to coat the cabbage with the hot oil, and immediately remove it from the heat.

Remove the chicken pieces from the serving dish, leaving the juices in the dish. Arrange the cabbage on top of the juices, and place the chicken on the cabbage. Warm the sauce, spoon it over the chicken and cabbage, and serve.

SUGGESTED ACCOMPANIMENT: *baked potatoes with chives and yogurt.*

Honey-Basil Chicken

Serves 4
Working time: 20 minutes
Total time: about 1 hour

Calories **258**
Protein **27g.**
Cholesterol **92mg.**
Total fat **12g.**
Saturated fat **3g.**
Sodium **215mg.**

4 whole chicken legs, skinned
¼ tsp. salt
freshly ground black pepper
1 tbsp. safflower oil
½ tbsp. unsalted butter
2 tbsp. honey
2 tbsp. unsalted chicken stock
2 garlic cloves, thinly sliced
30 to 40 fresh basil leaves

Preheat the oven to 400° F. Cut a piece of aluminum foil one foot square for each leg. Sprinkle the legs with the salt and pepper. Heat the oil and butter in a skillet over medium heat, then brown the legs for about two minutes on each side. Put a leg in the middle of each foil square, and drizzle 1 ½ teaspoons of the honey and 1 ½ teaspoons of the stock over each one. Lay one quarter of the garlic slices on each piece, cover with a loose layer of the basil leaves, and wrap the foil snugly over the top. Put the foil packages on a baking sheet and set it in the oven.

After 30 minutes, remove a foil package from the oven and unwrap it carefully to preserve the juices. Test for doneness by piercing the thigh with the tip of a sharp knife; if the juices run clear, it is done. If necessary, return the leg to the oven and bake about five minutes more.

To serve, undo each package and transfer the legs to a platter. Remove any garlic or basil that sticks to the foil and put them back on the chicken. Pour the collected juices from the foil packages over the legs.

SUGGESTED ACCOMPANIMENTS: *steamed carrots; romaine lettuce salad.*

Baked Chicken Breasts Stuffed with Tahini

SESAME PASTE, ALSO CALLED TAHINI, IS MADE FROM ROASTED
OR UNROASTED GROUND SESAME SEEDS. IT IS AVAILABLE IN JARS
OR CANS WHERE MIDDLE EASTERN FOODS ARE SOLD.

Serves 4
Working time: about 30 minutes
Total time: about 45 minutes

Calories **362**
Protein **32g.**
Cholesterol **73mg.**
Total fat **17g.**
Saturated fat **3g.**
Sodium **453mg.**

4 chicken breast halves, skinned and boned (about 1 lb.)
2 tbsp. sesame paste (tahini), or 2 tbsp. toasted sesame seeds, pulverized with a mortar and pestle
2 tbsp. chopped parsley
2 garlic cloves, finely chopped
1 tsp. fresh lemon juice
⅛ tsp. cayenne pepper
½ tsp. salt
freshly ground black pepper
2 tbsp. plain low-fat yogurt
2 tbsp. sesame seeds
½ cup dry bread crumbs
1½ tbsp. safflower oil
1 shallot, thinly sliced
¼ cup sherry
1 cup unsalted chicken stock
2 tsp. cornstarch, mixed with 1 tbsp. water
1 tomato, peeled, the outer flesh cut into strips

To make the tahini mixture, combine the sesame paste
or pulverized sesame seeds, parsley, garlic, lemon juice
and cayenne pepper in a small bowl. Cut a pocket in
each breast half: Make a horizontal slit along the
thicker long edge, beginning ½ inch from one end and
stopping ½ inch from the other. Then slice horizontally
into the breast, cutting to within ½ inch of the opposite edge to form a cavity bordered by ½ inch of uncut
flesh. Stuff one fourth of the tahini mixture into each
breast pocket. Sprinkle the chicken pieces with ¼ teaspoon of the salt and some pepper.

Preheat the oven to 350° F. To bread the pieces, first
coat them with the yogurt. Mix the sesame seeds with
the bread crumbs, and dredge the breasts in this mixture to coat them. Heat 1 tablespoon of the oil in a
heavy-bottomed skillet over medium heat. Cook the
chicken breasts until golden brown — about three
minutes per side.

Place the skillet in the oven and bake the breasts,
turning them once, until they feel firm but springy to
the touch — about 15 minutes. Transfer the chicken to
a serving platter and keep it warm.

For the sauce, heat the remaining ½ tablespoon of
oil in a small saucepan over medium-high heat. Sauté
the sliced shallot in the oil for one minute, then add the
sherry and reduce the mixture to about 1 tablespoon.
Pour in the stock and bring the liquid to a simmer. Stir
in the cornstarch mixture and cook for two minutes
more. Incorporate the tomato strips, the remaining ¼
teaspoon of salt and some pepper. Pour the sauce over
the stuffed breasts and serve.

SUGGESTED ACCOMPANIMENT: *cucumber salad with fresh mint.*

Baked Chicken Legs Stuffed with Millet

Serves 4
Working time: about 45 minutes
Total time: about 2 hours

Calories **406**
Protein **36g.**
Cholesterol **124mg.**
Total fat **24g.**
Saturated fat **8g.**
Sodium **347mg.**

4 chicken legs
1 tbsp. unsalted butter
1 onion, chopped
¼ cup millet
½ tsp. fresh rosemary, or ⅛ tsp. dried rosemary
¾ tsp. chopped fresh sage, or ¼ tsp. dried sage
½ cup unsalted chicken stock
⅛ tsp. salt
freshly ground black pepper
1 oz. prosciutto, cut in thin strips
2 oz. part-skim mozzarella, diced
2 tsp. safflower oil
2 tbsp. dry white wine

To make the stuffing, heat the butter over medium-low heat in a small, heavy-bottomed saucepan. Add the onion and cook until translucent — about five minutes. Add the millet, rosemary and sage, and cook for four minutes. Stir in the stock, salt and pepper, and bring to a boil. Reduce the heat to low, cover the pan, and simmer until the liquid is gone — about 20 minutes. The millet should be tender but not mushy. Empty this mixture into a small bowl and let it cool slightly before stirring in the prosciutto and mozzarella.

Meanwhile, place the legs skin side down on a work surface. Remove the thigh bone from each leg: Beginning at the end of the bone, gently scrape and cut the flesh away with the tip of a small, sharp knife, until you reach the joint. Pry the bone away from the joint and remove the bone. To make a pocket for the stuffing, start a cut at the channel left by the bone and work outward toward the edge of the thigh, stopping just short of slicing through to the skin. Repeat the process on the other side of the channel.

Mound stuffing onto the center of each thigh. Close

the meat back over the stuffing, wrapping the skin over the openings. Mold each thigh into a log shape and sew it up with a needle and butcher's twine. Preheat the oven to 350° F.

Heat the oil in a large, heavy-bottomed skillet over medium-high heat. Sauté the legs, skin side down, until they turn golden — about four minutes. Turn the pieces over and sauté them two minutes more. Transfer the legs to an ovenproof dish. Discard the fat and deglaze the skillet with the wine; pour the liquid over the chicken. Bake until the legs feel firm but springy to the touch — about 20 minutes. Serve immediately.

SUGGESTED ACCOMPANIMENT: *broiled tomatoes.*

Chicken Pillows

Serves 6
Working time: about 1 hour
Total time: about 1 hour and 30 minutes

Calories **348**
Protein **34g.**
Cholesterol **80mg.**
Total fat **16g.**
Saturated fat **4g.**
Sodium **352mg.**

6 chicken breast halves, skinned and boned, the long triangular fillets removed and reserved for another use, lightly pounded
2 tbsp. fresh lemon juice
3 tbsp. virgin olive oil
3 oz. part-skim mozzarella, cut into 6 slices
2 carrots, trimmed to 5 inches in length, cut into ¼-inch-wide strips and blanched in boiling water for three minutes
1 small yellow summer squash, trimmed to 5 inches in length, cut into ¼-inch-wide strips and blanched in boiling water for 30 seconds
6 thin asparagus spears (optional), trimmed to 5 inches in length and blanched in boiling water for one minute
6 scallions, trimmed to 5 inches in length and blanched in boiling water for one minute
½ cup fresh bread crumbs
1 garlic clove, finely chopped
⅛ tsp. salt
2 tbsp. finely chopped mixed fresh herbs, such as basil, parsley and chives
Tomato-garlic sauce
3 ripe tomatoes, peeled, seeded and coarsely chopped
2 garlic cloves, finely chopped
2 scallions, finely chopped
1 tbsp. virgin olive oil
¼ tsp. salt
freshly ground black pepper
4 tbsp. finely chopped fresh basil or parsley

Marinate the chicken breasts in the lemon juice and 1 tablespoon of the oil for one hour at room temperature, turning the pieces occasionally.

While the chicken is marinating, prepare the sauce. In a small, heavy-bottomed saucepan, combine the tomatoes, garlic, scallions, oil, salt and pepper. Bring the mixture to a boil over medium heat, then reduce the heat to medium low. Simmer the sauce until it thickens slightly — about 30 minutes. Remove the

sauce from the heat and stir in the basil or parsley. Preheat the oven to 375° F.

Remove the breasts from the marinade and place them smooth side down on a work surface. Reserve the marinade. Lay a slice of the mozzarella on each breast. Put one strip of each vegetable across the top. Roll up the breasts in loose packages and secure them with wooden picks. Arrange the chicken pillows in a baking dish. Brush them with the marinade and cover the dish with foil. Bake the chicken until it feels firm but springy to the touch — about 20 minutes.

While the breasts are baking, heat the remaining 2 tablespoons of oil in a small skillet over low heat and lightly brown the bread crumbs. Add the garlic, salt and mixed herbs.

Remove the chicken pillows from the oven and sprinkle them with the bread-crumb mixture. Broil until golden — two to three minutes. If necessary, reheat the sauce. Remove the picks, arrange the pillows on a warmed platter, and serve with the tomato sauce.

SUGGESTED ACCOMPANIMENT: *orzo or similar pasta.*

Spicy Yogurt-Baked Chicken Thighs

Serves 4
Working time: about 25 minutes
Total time: about 2 hours and 30 minutes

Calories **273**
Protein **31g.**
Cholesterol **102mg.**
Total fat **13g.**
Saturated fat **4g.**
Sodium **135mg.**

8 chicken thighs, skinned, fat removed
1 cup low-fat yogurt
2 tbsp. fresh lime juice
2 tsp. grated fresh ginger
4 garlic cloves, finely chopped
1 tsp. ground cumin
1 tsp. turmeric
½ tsp. cayenne pepper
1 tsp. anise seeds or fennel seeds, ground coarsely in a mortar and pestle
1 tsp. cornstarch, mixed with 2 tsp. water
1 lime, cut into wedges, for garnish

To prepare the marinade, combine the yogurt, lime juice, ginger, garlic and spices in a bowl and mix well. Place the chicken thighs in the marinade and stir to coat them. Cover the bowl and refrigerate it for two to eight hours. (The yogurt will tenderize as well as flavor the meat.) Preheat the oven to 350° F.

Arrange the thighs in a large, shallow baking dish, leaving no more than 1 inch of space between them; reserve the marinade. Bake for 10 minutes. Stir the cornstarch mixture into the marinade, then spread the mixture over the chicken pieces. Bake until the meat feels firm but springy to the touch — 10 to 15 minutes more. Transfer to a serving platter, arrange the lime wedges around the thighs, and serve.

SUGGESTED ACCOMPANIMENTS: *rice with raisins; chutney.*

Spinach-Stuffed Chicken Breasts

Serves 4
Working time: about 45 minutes
Total time: about 1 hour

Calories **431**
Protein **44g.**
Cholesterol **112mg.**
Total fat **22g.**
Saturated fat **9g.**
Sodium **684mg.**

4 chicken breast halves, boned, skin left on (about 1 lb.)
1 tsp. fresh thyme, or ¼ tsp. dried thyme leaves
¼ tsp. salt
1 tsp. virgin olive oil
Spinach and cheese stuffing
1 onion, finely chopped
1 tbsp. unsalted butter
1 tbsp. virgin olive oil
1 lb. spinach, washed, stemmed and coarsely chopped
½ cup low-fat ricotta cheese
½ cup freshly grated Parmesan cheese
1 tsp. fresh basil, finely chopped, or ½ tsp. dried basil
freshly ground black pepper
Yogurt-tomato sauce
1 cup plain low-fat yogurt
1 tbsp. red wine vinegar
¼ tsp. salt
1 ripe tomato, peeled, seeded and finely chopped
4 large basil leaves, thinly sliced
freshly ground black pepper

To prepare the stuffing, cook the onion in the butter and oil in a large, heavy-bottomed skillet over medium heat until translucent — about five minutes. Add the spinach to the pan and cook until it is wilted and the moisture has evaporated — about six minutes more. Transfer the mixture to a bowl and let it cool. Stir in the cheeses, basil and some pepper.

To make the sauce, mix the yogurt, vinegar and salt in a small bowl. Reserve 1 teaspoon of the tomato and 1 teaspoon of the basil, and stir the rest into the yogurt mixture. Add pepper to taste. Transfer the sauce to a serving bowl, garnish it with the reserved tomato and basil, and set it aside. Preheat the oven to 375° F.

To make pockets for the stuffing, loosen the skin of each breast by running a finger between the flesh and skin on one long side, leaving the skin attached on the other side. Rub the thyme and salt into the flesh. Drizzle ¼ teaspoon of the olive oil onto the skin of each breast. Neatly fill each pocket between skin and flesh with one quarter of the stuffing. Place the breasts skin side up in an oiled baking dish just large enough to hold them, and bake until the skin turns golden brown — about 25 minutes.

Remove the dish from the oven. Put the chicken breasts on a cutting board and allow them to cool for a few minutes. Cut each breast into ½-inch-wide slices and arrange them on a warmed serving platter or on individual plates. Serve with the yogurt sauce.

SUGGESTED ACCOMPANIMENT: *steamed couscous.*

Cajun Chicken Wings

Serves 4
Working time: about 20 minutes
Total time: about 1 hour

Calories **334**
Protein **28g.**
Cholesterol **87g.**
Total fat **21g.**
Saturated fat **6g.**
Sodium **353mg.**

12 chicken wings, tips removed
5 bay leaves, crumbled into small bits
¾ tsp. caraway seeds
½ to ¾ tsp. cayenne pepper
¾ tsp. ground coriander
¾ tsp. ground cumin
4 garlic cloves, finely chopped
1½ tsp. dry mustard
2 tsp. paprika
¾ tsp. dried thyme leaves
½ tsp. salt
2 tbsp. brandy
2 tbsp. fresh lemon or lime juice

Defat the chicken wings by cooking them in boiling water for 10 minutes. Drain, and set aside to cool. Preheat the oven to 375° F.

Using a large mortar and pestle, grind together the bay-leaf bits, caraway seeds, cayenne pepper, coriander, cumin, garlic, mustard, paprika, thyme and salt for about 10 minutes. Add the brandy and lemon or lime juice to the pulverized herbs, and stir into a thick paste.

With a pastry brush, cover both sides of each wing with the herb paste. When no more paste remains in the mortar, squeeze the last few drops from the brush. Arrange the chicken wings on a baking sheet.

Bake until the skin turns a deep brown and is quite crisp — 30 to 35 minutes.

SUGGESTED ACCOMPANIMENTS: *baked butternut squash; sautéed mushrooms.*

Chicken Wrapped in Crisp Phyllo

Serves 6
Working time: about 1 hour
Total time: about 1 day

Calories **500**
Protein **37g.**
Cholesterol **94mg.**
Total fat **27g.**
Saturated fat **7g.**
Sodium **547mg.**

6 chicken breast halves, skinned and boned (about 1½ lb.)
one 8-oz. box of phyllo dough
¾ tsp. salt
¾ tsp. freshly ground black pepper
4 tbsp. safflower oil
1 garlic clove, finely chopped
1 shallot, finely chopped
¾ lb. fresh spinach, washed and stemmed
¼ cup dry white wine
1 cup unsalted chicken stock
1 tbsp. heavy cream
2 oz. pistachio nuts, shelled, peeled and coarsely chopped (about ⅓ cup)
1 cup low-fat ricotta cheese

Defrost the frozen phyllo dough, unopened, in the refrigerator overnight; then leave it at room temperature for two hours before unwrapping it.

Slice each breast diagonally into three medallions. Sprinkle the pieces with ½ teaspoon each of the salt and pepper. Heat 1 tablespoon of the oil in a heavy-bottomed skillet over medium-high heat. Sear the chicken pieces for about 30 seconds on each side in several batches, adding as much as 2 additional tablespoons of oil as necessary between batches. Set the chicken aside on a plate.

Immediately add the garlic and shallot, and sauté them for about 30 seconds, stirring. Add the spinach, reduce the heat to low, and cover. Cook until the spinach is wilted — about two minutes. Remove the pan from the heat and take out half of the spinach mixture. Chop this finely and reserve it for the filling.

Heat the pan again over medium heat. Pour in the wine and stock, and stir to deglaze the pan. Stir in the remaining salt and pepper and the cream, and cook until the liquid is reduced by half. Purée the sauce in a blender. Pour it into a small saucepan and set it aside.

Preheat the oven to 325° F. To make the filling, combine the pistachios, ricotta and chopped spinach mixture. Gently blot the chicken medallions with paper towels to remove any excess juice. Unwrap the dough. Peel off a stack of three sheets and place them on a dry work surface. Cover the remaining sheets with a ▶

damp — not wet — paper towel to prevent them from drying out as you work.

Center a piece of chicken near an edge of the dough. Spread a thin layer of filling over the chicken, then top it with another medallion, a second layer of filling and a third chicken slice. Fold the sides of the dough over the chicken and roll it up. Place the roll seam side down in an oiled baking dish. Repeat with the remaining chicken pieces and phyllo sheets to make six rolls in all. Brush the rolls with the remaining tablespoon of oil.

Bake the rolls for 45 minutes. If additional baking is required to brown the phyllo, raise the temperature to 450° F. and keep the rolls in the oven a few minutes more. Warm the sauce and serve the rolls on top of it, as shown here, or pass it separately.

SUGGESTED ACCOMPANIMENT: *sautéed mushrooms and snow peas*.

Chicken-and-Cheese-Filled Calzones

THIS RECIPE WAS INSPIRED BY THE ITALIAN *CALZONE*, A KIND OF PIE MADE WITH PIZZA DOUGH.

Serves 4
Working time: about 1 hour
Total time: about 3 hours

Calories **626**
Protein **37g.**
Cholesterol **71mg.**
Total fat **22g.**
Saturated fat **6g.**
Sodium **589mg.**

two 6 oz. chicken breast halves, skinned and boned
1 tbsp. virgin olive oil
1 tbsp. cornmeal
Dough
2 packages active dry yeast or rapid-rise dry yeast
¼ tsp. sugar
2½ to 2¾ cups bread flour
½ tsp. salt
¼ tsp. fennel seeds, crushed
3 tbsp. virgin olive oil
Tomato and red pepper sauce
3 ripe tomatoes, peeled, seeded and chopped
1 red pepper, seeded, deribbed and chopped
1 onion, chopped
2 garlic cloves, finely chopped
¼ tsp. fennel seeds, crushed
1 tsp. fresh thyme, or ¼ tsp. dried thyme leaves
¾ tsp. chopped fresh oregano, or ¼ tsp. dried oregano
¼ tsp. salt
freshly ground black pepper
Cheese filling
¾ cup low-fat ricotta cheese
3 tbsp. freshly grated Parmesan cheese

To make the dough, pour ¼ cup of lukewarm water into a small bowl and sprinkle the yeast and sugar into it. Let stand for two to three minutes, then stir the mixture until the yeast and sugar are completely dissolved. Allow the mixture to sit in a warm place until the yeast bubbles up and the mixture has doubled in volume — three to five minutes.

Sift 2½ cups of the flour and the salt into a large bowl. Stir in the fennel seeds. Make a well in the center and pour in the yeast mixture, ¾ cup of lukewarm water and the oil. Mix the dough by hand; as soon as it can be gathered into a ball, place it on a floured board and add as much as needed of the additional ¼ cup flour if the dough is too soft and sticky. Knead until smooth and elastic — about 10 minutes.

To make the dough in a food processor, put the flour, salt and fennel seeds into the bowl of the processor and pulse twice to mix. Combine the yeast mixture with ¾ cup of lukewarm water and the oil. With the motor running, pour in the mixture as fast as the flour will absorb it; process until a ball of dough forms. Then process until the dough comes away from the sides of the bowl — about 40 seconds more.

Put the dough in a clean bowl and cover it with a towel. Set the bowl in a warm, draft-free place until the dough has doubled in size — about 1½ hours, or 45 minutes if you are using rapid-rise yeast.

To make the sauce, place the tomatoes, red pepper, onion, garlic, fennel seeds, thyme, oregano, salt and pepper in a large, heavy-bottomed saucepan. Simmer the mixture over medium heat, stirring frequently, until the liquid is absorbed — about 30 minutes. Remove from the heat and set aside.

Meanwhile, in a small bowl, mix the ricotta and Parmesan cheeses. Set aside. Preheat the oven to 475° F.

In a large, heavy-bottomed skillet, heat the oil over medium-high heat. Place the breasts in the skillet and sauté them for about two minutes on one side; turn and cook them on the other side — about two minutes more. (The meat should not be cooked through.) Remove the chicken from the heat and set aside.

Punch down the dough. Cut it into four equal pieces. Flatten each piece with the palm of the hand to produce a circle about 1 inch thick. Carefully stretch the dough by holding each round by its edge and rotating it with the fingers to obtain circles 6 inches in diameter. Alternatively, the dough can be stretched by patting it into a circle with the fingertips.

To assemble the calzones, place a chicken breast on each round of dough, a little off-center. Spread one quarter of the sauce on each breast and top with one quarter of the cheese filling. Moisten the inside edges of the dough with water and bring them up over the cheese to form a seal, and overlap the dough by ½ inch. Crimp the dough to close the calzones.

Place a baking sheet in the preheated oven for two minutes. Remove the pan from the oven and sprinkle the cornmeal on the areas on which the calzones will bake. Place the calzones on the cornmeal and brush the dough with the excess oil from the skillet. Bake until golden — 15 to 20 minutes.

SUGGESTED ACCOMPANIMENT: *spinach salad*.

Yogurt-Baked Chicken with Pimientos and Chives

Serves 4
Working time: about 20 minutes
Total time: about 2 hours and 30 minutes

Calories **321**
Protein **45g.**
Cholesterol **130mg.**
Total fat **11g.**
Saturated fat **4g.**
Sodium **322mg.**

one 3 lb. chicken, quartered, skinned and fat removed
1 cup plain low-fat yogurt
2 tbsp. finely cut fresh chives
¼ tsp. salt
¼ tsp. white pepper
1 tbsp. flour
1½ cups unsalted chicken stock
1 tbsp. very finely chopped pimiento

To prepare the marinade, combine the yogurt, chives, salt and pepper in a shallow dish. Add the chicken and marinate in the refrigerator for at least two hours.

Preheat the oven to 325° F. Transfer the chicken to a baking dish and reserve the marinade. Bake the chicken until the juices run clear when a thigh is pierced with the tip of a sharp knife — 25 to 30 minutes.

While the chicken is cooking, put the stock in a saucepan and bring it to a boil. Reduce the heat to maintain a slow simmer. Thoroughly mix the flour into the reserved marinade. Stir a few tablespoons of the hot stock into the marinade, then add the marinade to the stock, and simmer for three minutes. Add the pimiento and stir the sauce well.

Transfer the chicken from the baking dish to individual serving plates, and spoon the sauce over the pieces just before serving.

SUGGESTED ACCOMPANIMENTS: *lima beans; corn bread.*

Crepes Filled with Chicken and Corn

Serves 4
Working time: about 30 minutes
Total time: about 1 hour

Calories **385**
Protein **26g.**
Cholesterol **121mg.**
Total fat **17g.**
Saturated fat **5g.**
Sodium **415mg.**

2 chicken breast halves, skinned and boned (about ½ lb.), cut into ½-inch cubes
¼ tsp. salt
freshly ground black pepper
½ tsp. safflower oil

Crepe batter

1 to 1¼ cups skim milk
1 egg yolk (reserve white for filling)
¾ cup flour
1 tbsp. unsalted butter, melted
½ tsp. turmeric
⅛ tsp. salt
freshly ground black pepper
1 tsp. fresh thyme or ¼ tsp. dried thyme leaves
½ tsp. chopped parsley
½ tsp. chopped fresh tarragon or ¼ tsp. dried tarragon
½ tsp. chopped fresh mint
½ tsp. safflower oil for the crepe pan, if necessary

Corn filling and sauce

2 tbsp. safflower oil
1 shallot, chopped
1½ cups uncooked corn kernels (about 2 ears)
1 cup unsalted chicken stock
1 tbsp. heavy cream
½ cup low-fat cottage cheese
2 tbsp. cut fresh chives
1 egg white

To make the crepe batter, whisk together 1 cup of the milk and the egg yolk in a mixing bowl. Add the flour in small amounts, whisking continuously until all the flour has been incorporated and there are no lumps. Stir in the butter, turmeric, salt, pepper, thyme, parsley, tarragon and mint.

To make the crepes, heat a crepe pan or a 6-inch nonstick skillet over medium-high heat. If you are using a crepe pan, pour in ½ teaspoon of oil and wipe with a paper towel. Pour 2 to 3 tablespoons of the crepe batter into the hot pan and swirl it to just coat the bottom of the pan. Pour any excess back into the mixing bowl. Cook until brown — about 30 seconds — then lift the edge of the crepe and turn it over. Cook on the second side until brown — about 15 seconds more. Slide the crepe onto a plate. The crepe should be paper-thin; if it is not, add up to ¼ cup of the additional milk to the batter. Repeat the process with the remaining batter to make at least eight crepes, and set them aside. Preheat the oven to 325° F.

To prepare the crepe filling, sprinkle the chicken cubes with the salt and pepper. Heat 1 tablespoon of the oil in a heavy-bottomed skillet over medium-high heat. Sauté the chicken for four minutes and transfer it ▶

to a mixing bowl. Add the remaining tablespoon of oil to the skillet and sauté the shallot for 30 seconds. Add the corn and sauté for three minutes more. Remove ½ cup of the corn and add it to the chicken for the filling. To prepare the sauce, add the stock and the cream to the skillet, and simmer for three minutes. Then purée the mixture in a food processor or a blender.

Add the cottage cheese, 1 tablespoon of the chives, and the egg white to the bowl containing the chicken and corn, and mix well. Fill each crepe with about 4 tablespoons of this mixture, and roll it up. Wipe the inside of a baking dish with ½ teaspoon of oil. Place the rolled crepes seam side down in the dish and cover them with the sauce. Bake until the filling is heated through — about 20 minutes. Remove the crepes from the oven and garnish them with the remaining chives.

SUGGESTED ACCOMPANIMENT: *red leaf lettuce salad.*

Peach-Glazed Cornish Hens with Ginger

Serves 4
Working time: about 20 minutes
Total time: about 50 minutes

Calories **331**
Protein **23g.**
Cholesterol **44mg.**
Total fat **11g.**
Saturated fat **2g.**
Sodium **488mg.**

two 1½ lb. Cornish hens, halved, backbone removed
¾ cup orange juice
¼ lb. dried peaches, thinly sliced (about 1 cup)
2 tbsp. grated fresh ginger
1 tbsp. low-sodium soy sauce
1 tbsp. safflower oil
1 scallion, finely sliced
2 tbsp. brown sugar
1 tbsp. fresh lime juice
½ tsp. salt

Preheat the broiler. To make the glaze, combine the orange juice, peaches, ginger, soy sauce, safflower oil, scallion, brown sugar and lime juice in a small saucepan over medium heat. Cook, stirring once, for five minutes. Set the glaze aside.

Sprinkle the hens with the salt and put them skin side up on a broiler pan. To render some of their fat, place the hens under the broiler, close to the heat, and broil them until light brown — three to five minutes. Remove the hens from the broiler, discard the fat and set the oven temperature at 375° F. Coat the hens with the peach glaze and bake them for 25 minutes.

SUGGESTED ACCOMPANIMENT: *green beans with toasted almonds.*

Oven-Fried Cinnamon Chicken

Serves 4
Working time: about 15 minutes
Total time: about 1 hour

Calories **424**	one 3 lb. chicken, cut into four serving pieces and skinned
Protein **47g.**	½ tsp. salt
Cholesterol **125mg.**	½ tsp. freshly ground white pepper
Total fat **17g.**	¼ cup flour
Saturated fat **3g.**	¼ tsp. turmeric
Sodium **563mg.**	1 tsp. cinnamon
	3 egg whites
	1 cup fresh bread crumbs
	2 tbsp. safflower oil

Preheat the oven to 325° F. Mix the salt, pepper and flour, and spread on a plate. In a small bowl, whisk the turmeric and cinnamon into the egg whites. Dredge the chicken pieces in the flour, then dip them in the egg whites and coat them with the bread crumbs.

In a heavy-bottomed ovenproof skillet large enough to hold the chicken pieces in a single layer, heat the oil over medium heat. Lay the pieces bone side up in the skillet and brown them lightly on one side — about two minutes. Turn the pieces over, put the skillet in the oven, and bake for 30 minutes.

Remove the skillet and increase the oven temperature to 450° F. Wait about five minutes, then place the skillet in the oven and allow the coating to crisp for four or five minutes, taking care not to burn it.

SUGGESTED ACCOMPANIMENTS: *sautéed cherry tomatoes; green beans with tarragon.*

Chicken on a Bed of Savoy Cabbage

Serves 8
Working time: about 45 minutes
Total time: about 1 hour

Calories **397**
Protein **46g.**
Cholesterol **128mg.**
Total fat **16g.**
Saturated fat **4g.**
Sodium **366mg.**

two 3 lb. chickens, cut into serving pieces, all but the wings skinned
1 head Savoy cabbage (3 to 4 lb.)
⅓ cup whole-wheat flour
¼ tsp. cinnamon
1½ tbsp. safflower oil
½ tsp. salt
1 tbsp. virgin olive oil
3 ripe tomatoes, peeled, seeded and chopped
1 garlic clove, finely chopped
Curry sauce
2 carrots, thinly sliced
1½ cups plain low-fat yogurt
1 to 3 tsp. curry powder
1 tbsp. virgin olive oil
½ tsp. cinnamon
1 tbsp. honey
¼ tsp. salt

In order for its flavors to meld, make the sauce first. Cook the carrots in 1 cup of water in a small covered saucepan over medium heat until they are soft — about eight minutes. Drain the carrots and transfer them to a food processor or blender. Add 2 or 3 tablespoons of the yogurt and purée the mixture, scraping the sides down once. Add the remaining yogurt, 1 teaspoon of the curry powder, the olive oil, cinnamon, honey and salt, and purée again. Taste the sauce and blend in up to 2 teaspoons additional curry if desired. Transfer the sauce to a serving vessel and set it aside where it will stay lukewarm.

Discard any brown or wilted outer leaves of the cabbage. Slice the head into quarters, then cut out the core. Cut each quarter crosswise into three pieces, then separate the leaves and set them aside.

Preheat the oven to 400° F. Mix the flour with the cinnamon and coat the chicken pieces with this mixture. Heat 1 tablespoon of the safflower oil in a large, heavy-bottomed skillet over medium-high heat. Sauté half of the pieces on one side until brown — four to five minutes. Turn the pieces over and sprinkle them with ⅛ teaspoon of the salt. Sauté the chicken on the second side until brown — about four minutes more. Transfer the pieces to an ovenproof serving dish with their smooth sides facing up. Add the remaining ½ tablespoon of safflower oil to the skillet and sauté the remaining chicken pieces the same way. Arrange the pieces smooth sides up in the dish. Reserve the skillet for the tomatoes and cabbage.

Bake the chicken pieces until the juices run clear when a thigh is pierced with the tip of a sharp knife — 25 to 30 minutes.

While the chicken is baking, cook the cabbage. Pour enough water into a large pot to cover the bottom by about ½ inch. Set a vegetable steamer in the pot and put the cabbage in the steamer. Cover the pot tightly and bring the water to a boil. Steam the cabbage, uncovering it once to stir it, until it is wilted — five to seven minutes. Drain the cabbage well.

Heat the olive oil in the skillet over medium heat. Add the tomatoes and garlic, and cook for one minute. Stir in the cabbage and the remaining ¼ teaspoon of salt; toss well to heat the vegetables through. Set the skillet aside.

When the chicken is cooked, remove the pieces, leaving the juices in the serving dish. Arrange the cabbage and tomatoes in the bottom of the dish, then place the chicken on top. Serve the sauce separately.

SUGGESTED ACCOMPANIMENT: *steamed red potatoes with freshly cut chives.*

Lime-and-Mint Chicken

Serves 6
Working time: about 15 minutes
Total time: about 4 hours and 15 minutes

Calories **248**
Protein **27g.**
Cholesterol **98mg.**
Total fat **12g.**
Saturated fat **3g.**
Sodium **183mg.**

12 chicken thighs, skinned
½ tsp. sugar
Lime marinade
1 cup fresh lime juice
⅓ cup dry white wine
¾ cup chopped fresh mint leaves, plus 6 whole mint sprigs reserved for garnish
1½ tsp. cumin seeds, crushed, or ¾ tsp. ground cumin
3 scallions, thinly sliced
1 large dried red chili, seeded and thinly sliced (see caution, page 25), or ½ to ¾ tsp. crushed red pepper
¼ tsp. salt

Combine the marinade ingredients in a shallow bowl or dish large enough to hold the chicken thighs. Put the thighs in the bowl and coat them with the marinade. Cover the bowl with a lid or plastic wrap and refrigerate it for four to six hours.

Preheat the broiler. Remove the chicken from the marinade and arrange the pieces in a broiler pan. Strain the marinade into a small bowl and reserve both the strained liquid and the drained mint mixture. Broil the chicken 4 to 6 inches below the heat source until it is browned — six to eight minutes. Remove the pan from the oven and turn the pieces over. Spoon some of the mint mixture over each thigh. Broil the thighs until the juices run clear when a piece is pierced with the tip of a sharp knife — six to eight minutes more.

While the chicken is broiling on the second side, stir the sugar into the strained marinade. Put the liquid in a small saucepan and boil it over high heat for two minutes, stirring frequently, to produce a light sauce.

To serve, spoon some of the sauce over each thigh and garnish with the mint sprigs.

SUGGESTED ACCOMPANIMENTS: *baked sweet potatoes; steamed cauliflower.*

Saffron Chicken with Yogurt

Serves 6
Working time: about 30 minutes
Total time: about 1 day

Calories **210**
Protein **28g.**
Cholesterol **91mg.**
Total fat **9g.**
Saturated fat **2g.**
Sodium **185mg.**

6 whole chicken legs, skinned
¼ cup unsalted chicken stock
⅛ tsp. saffron (about 20 threads)
¼ tsp. salt
freshly ground black pepper
½ cup low-fat yogurt
½ cup chopped onion
2 garlic cloves, finely chopped
1 tsp. grated fresh ginger
¼ cup fresh lemon juice
⅛ tsp. cayenne pepper
¼ tsp. ground cumin

Combine the stock and saffron in a small saucepan over medium heat and bring them to a simmer. Remove the pan from the heat and let the saffron steep for about five minutes. The stock will turn golden.

Sprinkle the chicken legs with the salt and pepper. Put them in a shallow baking dish and drizzle the stock-and-saffron mixture over them. Turn the legs to coat both sides and arrange them so that they do not touch.

Combine the yogurt, onion, garlic, ginger, lemon juice, cayenne pepper and cumin in a food processor or blender, and purée. Pour the mixture over the chicken and cover with a sheet of plastic wrap. Refrigerate for

eight hours or overnight.

Preheat the broiler. Remove the legs from the marinade and arrange them top side down in a foil-lined broiler pan. Reserve the marinade for basting. Position the broiler pan 3½ to 4 inches below the heat source. Broil the legs for about eight minutes on each side, basting them with the marinade every two minutes. The chicken is done when the juices run clear from a thigh pierced with the tip of a sharp knife.

SUGGESTED ACCOMPANIMENTS: *toasted pita bread; grated carrot salad.*

Broiled Chicken with Malt Vinegar and Basil

Serves 4
Working time: about 30 minutes
Total time: about 1 day

Calories **281**
Protein **30g.**
Cholesterol **105mg.**
Total fat **15g.**
Saturated fat **4g.**
Sodium **233mg.**

4 whole chicken legs, skinned
¾ cup malt vinegar
½ cup dry white wine
2 large shallots, thinly sliced
2 tsp. ground mace
freshly ground black pepper
2 tbsp. chopped fresh basil leaves, or 2 tsp. dried basil
¼ tsp. salt

To prepare the marinade, combine the vinegar, wine, shallots, mace, pepper and basil in a saucepan. Bring the mixture to a simmer over medium heat and cook for two minutes. Sprinkle the chicken legs with the salt and set them in a shallow baking dish. Pour the marinade over the chicken and cover the dish with plastic wrap. Refrigerate for eight hours or overnight.

Preheat the broiler. Remove the legs from the marinade and arrange them on a foil-lined broiler pan. Reserve the marinade for basting. Broil the legs 3½ to 4 inches below the heat source for about eight minutes on each side, brushing them with the marinade every four minutes. The chicken is done when the juices run clear from a thigh pierced with the tip of a sharp knife.

SUGGESTED ACCOMPANIMENTS: *boiled new potatoes; steamed red cabbage.*

Chicken Breasts with Radishes

Serves 4
Working time: about 30 minutes
Total time: about 1 day

Calories **216**
Protein **27g.**
Cholesterol **72mg.**
Total fat **4g.**
Saturated fat **2g.**
Sodium **202mg.**

4 chicken breast halves, skinned and boned, the wings severed at the second joint from the tip
¼ tsp. salt
6 large radishes, thinly sliced
1 cup red wine vinegar
½ cup dry white wine
1 ½ tbsp. chopped fresh tarragon leaves, or ½ tbsp. dried tarragon
freshly ground black pepper
2 tbsp. honey

Sprinkle both sides of the breasts with the salt. With the knife held perpendicular to the long edge of a breast, cut diagonally into the smooth side of the flesh to make four ½-inch-deep slits at ¾-inch intervals across the breast. Cut similar diagonal slits in the other

breasts. Cover the bottom of a shallow dish with the radishes and lay the breasts, cut side down, on top.

To prepare the marinade, combine the vinegar, wine, tarragon, pepper and honey in a saucepan. Bring the liquid to a simmer over medium heat, and cook for two minutes. Stir the marinade and pour it over the breasts. Cover the dish with plastic wrap and refrigerate it for eight hours or overnight.

Preheat the broiler when you are ready to cook the chicken. Arrange the breasts cut side down in a foil-lined broiler pan. Reserve the marinade for basting.

Broil the chicken 3½ to 4 inches below the heat source for four minutes on the first side, basting once. Turn the breasts and broil them on the second side for two minutes. Remove the breasts from the broiler and tuck one, two or three radish slices into each of the slits, forming a fish-scale pattern. Broil the chicken for another two minutes. Make a small cut in the thick portion of a breast to see if the meat has turned white. If it is still pink, broil it for one or two minutes more.

Pour the accumulated cooking juices over the chicken breasts and serve.

SUGGESTED ACCOMPANIMENT: *watercress and red onion salad.*

Chicken Thighs Broiled with Sherry and Honey

Serves 4
Working time: about 20 minutes
Total time: about 25 minutes

Calories **338**
Protein **28g.**
Cholesterol **98mg.**
Total fat **11g.**
Saturated fat **3g.**
Sodium **384mg.**

8 chicken thighs, skinned
1 cup dry sherry
3 tbsp. honey
4 garlic cloves, finely chopped
3 tbsp. red wine vinegar
1 tbsp. low-sodium soy sauce
1 tbsp. cornstarch, mixed with 2 tbsp. dry sherry
¼ tsp. salt

Boil the sherry in a small saucepan until it is reduced by half — about seven minutes. Remove the pan from the stove and whisk in the honey, garlic, vinegar and soy sauce. Return the pan to the heat and whisk the cornstarch mixture into the sauce. Bring the sauce to a boil and cook for one minute, whisking constantly. Remove the pan from the heat and let the sauce cool.

Preheat the broiler. Sprinkle the salt on both sides of the thighs and lay them bone side up on a rack in a roasting pan. Brush the chicken pieces liberally with the sauce, then broil them 4 to 6 inches from the heat source for six to seven minutes. Turn them over and brush them again with the sauce. Broil the thighs for three or four minutes more, then brush them again with the remaining sauce. Continue broiling until the juices run clear when a thigh is pierced with the tip of a sharp knife — five to seven minutes more. Transfer the chicken pieces to a platter and trickle any remaining sauce from the roasting pan over them.

SUGGESTED ACCOMPANIMENT: *snow peas sautéed with water chestnuts and soy sauce.*

Dry-Martini Cornish Hens

Serves 4
Working time: about 30 minutes
Total time: 1 to 2 days

Calories **299**
Protein **28g.**
Cholesterol **88mg.**
Total fat **14g.**
Saturated fat **4g.**
Sodium **360mg.**

four 1 lb. Cornish hens, giblets reserved for another use, cavities washed and patted dry
2 tbsp. juniper berries, crushed
zest of 2 lemons, cut into ¼-inch-wide strips
2 cups unsalted chicken stock
¾ cup gin
¼ cup dry vermouth
½ tsp. salt
freshly ground black pepper

To make the marinade, combine the juniper berries, lemon zest, 1½ cups of the stock, ½ cup of the gin, the vermouth, salt and pepper in a small bowl. Place the hens in a deep dish that holds them snugly, and pour the marinade over them. Swirl some of the marinade into the cavity of each bird. Cover the dish with a lid or plastic wrap, and refrigerate it for 24 to 48 hours. Turn the hens from time to time as they marinate.

Preheat the oven to 375° F. Remove the birds from the marinade and put 1 tablespoon of the marinade liquid, a few of the crushed juniper berries and some of the lemon zest in the cavity of each bird. Discard the remaining marinade. Tie each pair of legs together with butcher's twine. Arrange the hens breast side up on the rack of a roasting pan so that they do not touch. Roast them until they are golden brown — 40 to 45 minutes. Pour the juices, juniper berries and lemon zest from the cavity of each hen into the roasting pan, and set the birds on a warmed serving platter.

To make the sauce, remove the rack and place the roasting pan over medium-high heat. Add the remaining ½ cup of stock and the remaining ¼ cup of gin. Cook the sauce, stirring with a wooden spoon to dislodge any brown bits, until the liquid is reduced by about half and has thickened — seven to 10 minutes. Strain the sauce and serve it with the hens. Garnish the birds, if you like, with twists of freshly cut lemon peel.

SUGGESTED ACCOMPANIMENTS: *steamed baby carrots; red potatoes.*

Cornish Hens with Pineapple and Mint

Serves 4
Working time: about 1 hour
Total time: about 1 hour and 30 minutes

Calories **424**
Protein **27g.**
Cholesterol **52mg.**
Total fat **11g.**
Saturated fat **4g.**
Sodium **331mg.**

two 1 ½ lb. Cornish hens, neck, gizzard and heart reserved
1 cup bulgur, rinsed and drained
1 pineapple, peeled and cored
2 navel oranges, the zest of one grated and reserved for the stuffing
2 scallions, sliced into thin rounds
½ cup chopped fresh mint, a few whole sprigs reserved for garnish
½ tsp. salt
freshly ground black pepper
1 tbsp. unsalted butter
8 garlic cloves, unpeeled
¼ cup dry white wine

Put the bulgur in a small bowl and add enough boiling water to cover. Let the bulgur soak for 10 minutes. Empty the bowl into a sieve to drain the bulgur. Cut a few slices from the pineapple and reserve them for use as a garnish. Coarsely chop the rest of the pineapple in a food processor or by hand. Cook the chopped pineapple in a skillet over medium-low heat until the juices have evaporated — 20 to 25 minutes.

Meanwhile, prepare each hen: Starting at the neck, use your fingers to separate the skin from either side of the breast. Then, with a knife, cut through the membrane attaching the skin to the breast, taking care not to puncture the skin. Remove and discard any bits of fat. Preheat the oven to 450° F.

To prepare the stuffing, first segment one of the oranges: Cut away the peel with a knife, cutting deep enough to remove the bitter white pith and expose the flesh. Then hold the orange over a bowl to catch its juice as you slice down to the core on either side of each segment. Dislodge the segments and let them fall into the bowl as you proceed. Cut the second orange in half and squeeze its juice into the bowl. Remove the orange segments from the juice and cut them into small pieces; reserve the juice for the sauce. Combine the orange pieces, the bulgur and the chopped pineapple in a mixing bowl. Mix in the scallions, mint, salt, some pepper and the orange zest.

Gently push about ½ cup of the stuffing under the skin of each bird, molding the skin into a smooth, round shape. Tuck the neck flap under each bird. Reserve the extra stuffing in a small ovenproof bowl or baking dish, and cover it with foil.

Melt the butter in a small pan over medium-low heat. Place the hens on an oiled rack in a roasting pan.

Distribute the neck, gizzard, heart and garlic cloves in the bottom of the pan. Brush the birds with some of the butter and roast them in the upper third of the oven for 15 minutes. Baste them with the remaining butter and any accumulated pan juices, and return them to the oven along with the reserved stuffing. Roast until the hens are golden brown and the juices run clear when a thigh is pierced with the tip of a sharp knife — 20 to 25 minutes more.

Remove the birds from the oven and turn it off, leaving the stuffing inside while you prepare the sauce. Remove the rack, garlic and giblets from the pan, and skim off the fat. Reserve the giblets for later use in the stockpot. Set the pan over medium heat and stir in the orange juice and wine to deglaze it. Squeeze the garlic cloves from their skins and add them to the sauce. Simmer and stir for one minute. Pour the sauce through a sieve set over a small bowl. Press the soft garlic through the sieve with a wooden spoon and stir the sauce well.

Cut each bird in half lengthwise, and set the halves on a platter or on individual plates. Arrange the warm stuffing around each bird and spoon the sauce over the top. Garnish with the whole mint sprigs and raw pineapple, and serve hot.

SUGGESTED ACCOMPANIMENT: *steamed kale.*

Roast Capon with Sage Corn Bread Stuffing

Serves 8
Working time: about 45 minutes
Total time: about 2 hours and 15 minutes

Calories **444**	one 9 to 10 lb. capon, rinsed and patted dry
Protein **42g.**	1 tbsp. unsalted butter
Cholesterol **110mg.**	4 large onions, thinly sliced
Total fat **21g.**	1 tbsp. safflower oil
Saturated fat **5g.**	½ tsp. salt
Sodium **345mg.**	1½ oz. boiled ham, cut into small cubes
	½ cup unsalted chicken stock

Sage corn bread
1 cup yellow cornmeal
1 cup flour
1 tbsp. baking powder
¼ tsp. salt
¼ tsp. freshly ground black pepper
1 cup buttermilk
1 egg, beaten
2 tbsp. safflower oil
2 tbsp. chopped fresh sage, or 1½ tsp. dried sage

Preheat the oven to 425° F.

To prepare the corn bread, combine the cornmeal, flour, baking powder, salt and pepper. Stir in the buttermilk, egg, oil and sage. Pour the batter into a lightly oiled 8-by-8-inch baking pan and bake until golden brown — 20 to 25 minutes. Reduce the oven temperature to 375° F.

Meanwhile, melt the butter in a heavy-bottomed saucepan over medium-low heat. Add the onions and cook for 20 minutes, stirring occasionally. Add the tablespoon of oil and cook until the onions are caramelized — about 40 minutes more. Scrape the bottom often to avoid sticking and burning.

While the onions are cooking, truss the capon as shown on page 138. Place a metal steamer or rack in the bottom of a large stockpot, and pour in enough water to cover the bottom by about 1 inch. Bring the water to a boil, then place the bird in the pot and cover it tightly. Steam for 20 minutes over high heat. Remove the capon, sprinkle its skin immediately with ¼ teaspoon of the salt, and let the bird stand while you prepare the stuffing.

Crumble the corn bread into a bowl and stir in the caramelized onions, ham and chicken stock. Pour off any juices from the cavity of the bird and sprinkle the inside with the remaining ¼ teaspoon of salt. Fill the capon loosely with the stuffing, and cover the opening with a small piece of aluminum foil. Place any excess stuffing in a small ovenproof dish, moisten it with a little chicken stock, cover with foil and bake along with the capon during the last 20 minutes of roasting time. Put the bird breast side up on a rack in a roasting pan. Roast the capon until the skin is crisp and golden and the juices run clear when a thigh is pierced with the tip of a sharp knife — about one hour and 10 minutes.

SUGGESTED ACCOMPANIMENTS: *sautéed apples; mashed rutabaga.*

EDITOR'S NOTE: *The process of steaming followed by roasting helps to defat the capon considerably, resulting in a crisp skin and fewer calories.*

Roast Chicken with Apples, Turnips and Garlic

Serves 4
Working time: about 30 minutes
Total time: about 1 hour and 30 minutes

Calories **378**
Protein **39g.**
Cholesterol **103mg.**
Total fat **17g.**
Saturated fat **5g.**
Sodium **197mg.**

one 3 lb. chicken
1 tbsp. paprika
½ tsp. freshly ground black pepper
⅛ tsp. salt
1 tsp. unsalted butter
2 or 3 Golden Delicious apples, peeled, cored and cut into eighths
3 small white turnips, peeled, quartered and thinly sliced
6 garlic cloves, peeled
juice of half a lemon

Preheat the oven to 325° F. Mix the paprika, pepper and salt, and rub the chicken inside and out with them.

Butter a roasting pan and put the chicken in it. Arrange the apples, turnips and garlic around the bird. Trickle the lemon juice over the top of the apples and turnips. Roast the chicken until it is golden brown all over and a leg moves easily when wiggled up and down — 65 to 75 minutes. Baste the bird with the pan juices two or three times during the cooking.

When the chicken is done, skim the fat from the pan and mash the apples, turnips and garlic together with the pan juices. Serve in a separate bowl.

SUGGESTED ACCOMPANIMENT: *sugar-snap peas.*

Thyme-Roasted Chicken

Serves 4
Working time: about 30 minutes
Total time: about 1 hour and 30 minutes

Calories **294**
Protein **38g.**
Cholesterol **82mg.**
Total fat **12g.**
Saturated fat **4g.**
Sodium **382mg.**

one 3½ to 4 lb. chicken, giblets reserved for another use, rinsed and patted dry
½ tsp. salt
freshly ground black pepper
1 tbsp. fresh thyme leaves, stems reserved for flavoring the cavity
6 to 8 bay leaves, crumbled into small bits
½ cup dry white wine

Season the body cavity with ⅛ teaspoon of the salt and some pepper. Working from the edge of the cavity, gently lift the skin covering the breast, taking care not to tear it, and distribute the thyme leaves under the skin so that they evenly cover the meat. Let the skin fall back into place. Place the thyme stems and the bay leaves in the cavity. Prepare the chicken for roasting by trussing it as demonstrated on page 138. Preheat the oven to 400° F.

Select a stockpot that has a tight-fitting lid and is large enough to accommodate the chicken. Fill the pot 1 inch deep with water. Place the chicken in the pot on a rack high enough to hold the bird clear of the water. Set the pot over high heat, cover tightly, and steam the chicken for 15 minutes to begin to render its fat.

Carefully remove the bird from the pot and transfer it to the rack of a roasting pan. Quickly season the outside of the bird with the remaining salt and some pepper. Roast the chicken until it is a light golden brown all over — 40 to 45 minutes.

Remove the chicken and pour the contents of its cavity into the roasting pan. Add the white wine and 1 cup of water. Place the pan over medium heat and simmer the liquid, scraping up any pan deposits, until it is reduced by half — seven to 10 minutes.

Carve the chicken and arrange the meat on a warmed platter. Strain the reduced sauce, and spoon it over the chicken.

SUGGESTED ACCOMPANIMENT: *julienned carrots steamed with currants.*

EDITOR'S NOTE: *The process of steaming followed by roasting helps to defat the chicken considerably, resulting in a crisp, savory skin and fewer calories. As an alternative to the thyme leaves, 1 tablespoon of fresh rosemary or sage leaves or ¼ cup of chopped fresh basil leaves may be inserted between the skin and breast; the stems of these herbs may be placed in the cavity for additional aromatic flavoring.*

Emerald Chicken Roll

SO THAT THE CHICKEN WILL HAVE THE PROPER TEXTURE, ALL MEMBRANES AND CARTILAGE MUST BE REMOVED BEFORE THE MEAT IS PURÉED. CHICKEN BREASTS ARE EASIER TO USE THAN LEGS OR THIGHS.

Serves 8
Working time: about 45 minutes
Total time: about 1 hour and 15 minutes

Calories **146**
Protein **18g.**
Cholesterol **50mg.**
Total fat **6g.**
Saturated fat **3g.**
Sodium **150mg.**

1 lb. chicken meat, cut into 2-inch pieces
¼ oz. dried mushrooms
12 to 15 large romaine lettuce leaves
1 tbsp. chopped parsley
½ tsp. fresh tarragon leaves, or ½ tsp. dried tarragon
2 scallions, green stalks trimmed to within 2 inches of the white part, cut into pieces
½ tsp. ground coriander
¼ tsp. salt
freshly ground black pepper
1 cup low-fat ricotta cheese
½ cup unsalted chicken stock
1 egg white
½ tbsp. cornstarch, mixed with 2 tbsp. Madeira or port wine
1 tbsp. unsalted butter
2 tbsp. finely cut fresh chives

Put the mushrooms in a small bowl and pour 1¼ cups of boiling water over them. Cover, and set aside for 30 minutes. Meanwhile, place the lettuce leaves in a large pot with a tight-fitting lid and pour ½ cup of cold water over them. Place a piece of aluminum foil directly on top of the lettuce and cover. Bring the water to a boil and steam the leaves for one minute to make them limp. Remove the pan from the heat and take off the lid and foil. When the leaves are cool enough to handle, cut out the thick core at the base of each stem. Spread the leaves on paper towels to drain.

Put the chicken in the bowl of a food processor. Add the parsley, tarragon, scallion, coriander, salt and a generous grinding of pepper. Process in short bursts until the chicken is coarsely chopped. Add the ricotta and chicken stock, and purée until smooth. Scrape down the sides of the bowl; then, with the motor running, add the egg white and process until it is thoroughly incorporated — about five seconds more.

Remove the mushrooms from the water and squeeze them gently over the bowl to rid them of excess water; strain and reserve the soaking liquid. Chop the mushrooms into coarse pieces and add them to the processor bowl. Using a few short bursts, process just enough to incorporate the mushrooms into the chicken mixture. Poach a spoonful of the mixture in simmering water; taste and correct the seasonings, if necessary.

Spread a piece of plastic wrap about 18 inches long on a work surface. Lay the lettuce leaves one by one in a row, each long edge overlapping the next, to form a rectangle roughly 16 inches long and 8 inches wide. Spoon the chicken mixture in a row lengthwise down the center of the lettuce rectangle. Use a rubber spat- ▶

ula dipped in cold water to shape the mixture into a log. Pull up the lettuce leaves on each side to cover the chicken, then roll the log in the plastic wrap, tucking the ends of the plastic underneath. Make three small slashes in the plastic wrap on the top of the roll to allow steam to escape.

Add enough water to the mushroom-soaking liquid to total 1½ cups. Pour the liquid into a fish poacher or wok (or other pot large enough to hold the roll) fitted with a rack or steamer. Place the chicken roll on the rack. Cover, and steam the roll until it feels firm to the touch — about 25 minutes. Lift the roll out of the steamer and set it aside. Remove the rack.

Stir the cornstarch mixture into the simmering liquid. Cook until the sauce is translucent and somewhat thick — about one minute. Remove the pot from the heat. Add the butter, and swirl the sauce until the butter melts. Stir the chives into the sauce.

Unwrap the chicken roll, letting any accumulated juices run into the sauce. Cut the roll into diagonal slices about ¾ inch thick and arrange them on a serving platter. Pour the sauce into a heated sauceboat and pass it separately.

SUGGESTED ACCOMPANIMENTS: *julienned carrots; tomato salad.*

EDITOR'S NOTE: *The chicken mixture may be rolled in individual lettuce leaves, allowing about ⅓ cup of the mixture for each roll. The steaming procedure remains the same, but the time should be reduced to 15 minutes.*

Cold Chicken and Asparagus with Lemon-Tarragon Vinaigrette

Serves 4
Working time: about 45 minutes
Total time: about 45 minutes

Calories **280**
Protein **29g.**
Cholesterol **72mg.**
Total fat **15g.**
Saturated fat **2g.**
Sodium **135mg.**

4 chicken breast halves, skinned and boned (about 1 lb.)
20 asparagus spears, bottom ends trimmed, and peeled ⅓ of the way up the stalks
½ tsp. safflower oil
⅛ tsp. salt
freshly ground black pepper
½ red pepper, julienned
Lemon-tarragon vinaigrette
1 tbsp. chopped shallot, or 2 scallions, finely chopped
3 tbsp. fresh lemon juice
½ tsp. fresh thyme, or ⅛ tsp. dried thyme leaves
1½ tsp. chopped fresh tarragon, or ½ tsp. dried tarragon
2 tbsp. safflower oil
1 tbsp. virgin olive oil
1 garlic clove, chopped
1 tbsp. chopped fresh parsley
1 tsp. sugar
freshly ground black pepper

To make the vinaigrette, combine the shallot or scallions, lemon juice, thyme and tarragon. Let stand for 10 minutes, then whisk in the safflower and olive oils and the garlic, parsley, sugar and pepper. Allow to stand for 10 minutes more.

In a heavy-bottomed skillet, heat the safflower oil over very low heat. Sprinkle the breasts with the salt and pepper. Place the breasts in the skillet and cover them with a heavy plate to weight them down and preserve their juices. Cook the breasts on one side for five minutes, turn, and cook for another three to four minutes. The meat should feel firm but springy to the touch, and there should be no visible pink along the edges. Remove from the skillet and cool in the refrigerator for at least 10 minutes or until ready to serve.

To cook the asparagus, place the stalks in a skillet with ¼ cup of water. Cover, bring to a boil, and cook until the asparagus are tender but still crisp — about two minutes. Drain, rinse under cold running water to stop the cooking, chill, and keep cool.

Slice the breasts on the diagonal and arrange each one on an individual serving plate with five asparagus spears. Garnish with the red pepper and spoon the vinaigrette over the chicken and asparagus.

SUGGESTED ACCOMPANIMENT: *French bread.*

Spatchcocked Chicken with Basil-Yogurt Sauce

THE WORD "SPATCHCOCK" COMES FROM THE IRISH TERM "DISPATCH COCK," A DISH FOR A SUDDEN OCCASION. HERE IT REFERS TO A WHOLE CHICKEN THAT IS SPLIT OPEN AND FLATTENED FOR EVEN COOKING.

Serves 4
Working time: about 25 minutes
Total time: about 1 hour and 15 minutes

Calories **392**
Protein **45g.**
Cholesterol **91mg.**
Total fat **20g.**
Saturated fat **6g.**
Sodium **367mg.**

one 3 lb. chicken, rinsed and patted dry
1 cup plain low-fat yogurt
1 cup fresh basil leaves, chopped, or 2 cups fresh spinach leaves, lightly steamed and squeezed dry
3 scallions, chopped
2 garlic cloves, finely chopped
1 tbsp. virgin olive oil
⅓ cup freshly grated Parmesan or Romano cheese
⅛ tsp. salt
freshly ground black pepper

Prepare the bird for roasting as demonstrated in the steps below. Preheat the oven to 400° F. Cover the bottom of a large pot with 1 inch of water. Set a steamer or rack in the pot, and bring the water to a boil. Place the chicken skin side up on the steamer. Cover tightly and steam the chicken for 15 minutes over high heat.

While the chicken is steaming, make the sauce. Combine the yogurt, basil or spinach, scallions, garlic, oil and half of the Parmesan or Romano cheese in a food processor or blender. Process until smooth, then transfer the sauce to a sauceboat and set it aside at room temperature.

Set the steamed chicken on a rack in a roasting pan.

Sprinkle it with the salt and some pepper. Roast until the skin is a crispy, light brown — about 25 minutes.

Remove the bird from the oven and sprinkle the remaining cheese over it. Return the chicken to the oven and roast until the cheese is golden brown — eight to 10 minutes more.

Allow the chicken to stand 10 minutes, then carve it into serving pieces. Pass the sauce separately.

SUGGESTED ACCOMPANIMENTS: *stewed tomatoes; brown rice.*

EDITOR'S NOTE: *The process of steaming followed by roasting helps to defat the chicken considerably, resulting in a crisp skin and fewer calories.*

Spatchcocking a Chicken

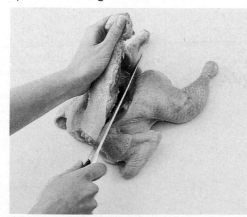

1 REMOVING THE BACKBONE. *Place a whole chicken breast side down on a work surface. With a heavy chef's knife, cut down along one side of the backbone from the tail toward the neck, using a sawing motion to cut through the rib cage. Repeat this process on the other side and pull the backbone free.*

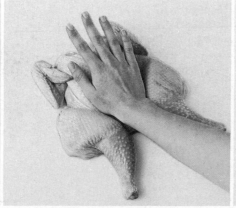

2 FLATTENING THE BIRD. *Turn the bird breast side up, with its drumsticks pointed toward you. Then, with one forceful motion, press the heel of your hand down on the breastbone to flatten out the breast. Tuck the wing tips behind the chicken's shoulders.*

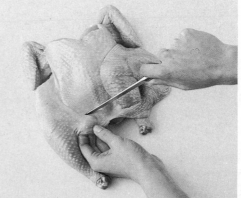

3 SECURING THE DRUMSTICKS. *To keep the drumsticks from spreading out as the bird cooks, tuck them into a flap of skin: First pull the skin around the tail cavity taut, then cut a slit about ¾ inch long between a thigh and the tapered end of the breast. Thread the end of the drumstick through the slit. Repeat the procedure to secure the second leg.*

tablespoon of lime juice and a generous grinding of pepper. Using a slotted spoon, transfer the pieces to a bowl. Refrigerate them for at least 10 minutes.

Whisk the remaining 2 tablespoons of oil into the dressing mixture. Remove the couscous and the chicken from the refrigerator. Stir the dressing into the couscous. Finally, add the chicken, the remaining scallions and the red pepper, and mix well. Serve each portion on a bed of lettuce.

SUGGESTED ACCOMPANIMENT: *sliced tomatoes.*

Chilled Chicken Couscous with Lime

Serves 4
Working time: about 30 minutes
Total time: about 40 minutes

Calories **435**
Protein **23g.**
Cholesterol **57mg.**
Total fat **18g.**
Saturated fat **3g.**
Sodium **214mg.**

¾ lb. chicken meat, cut into ¾-inch pieces (about 1 ½ cups)
2 tbsp. finely chopped onion
4 tbsp. safflower oil
1 cup couscous
1 cup unsalted chicken stock
5 tbsp. fresh lime juice
1 garlic clove, finely chopped
4 tsp. fresh thyme, or 1 tsp. dried thyme leaves
¼ tsp. salt
freshly ground black pepper
6 scallions, trimmed and finely chopped
1 red pepper, seeded, deribbed and chopped into ½-inch squares
lettuce leaves (for serving)

In a heavy-bottomed skillet with a tight-fitting lid, sauté the onion in 1 tablespoon of the oil over medium-high heat for about two minutes. Stir in the couscous, the stock and 1 cup of water, and boil rapidly for about two minutes. Remove the skillet from the heat and cover it; let it stand for five minutes. Remove the lid, fluff up the couscous with a fork, and transfer the mixture to a large mixing bowl. Put the bowl in the refrigerator to cool.

For the dressing, combine 4 tablespoons of the lime juice, the garlic, thyme, salt and some pepper. Add half the scallions and set the mixture aside.

Add another tablespoon of oil to the skillet and set it over high heat. When the oil is hot, add the chicken pieces and sauté them, stirring frequently, until lightly browned — four to five minutes. Stir in the remaining

Sage-Flavored Chicken Pot Pie with Phyllo Crust

Serves 4
Working time: about 1 hour
Total time: about 1 hour and 30 minutes

Calories **438**
Protein **26g.**
Cholesterol **70mg.**
Total fat **17g.**
Saturated fat **6g.**
Sodium **368mg.**

¾ lb. boneless chicken meat, skinned and cut into ½-inch cubes (from about 5 large thighs or 3 breast halves)
1 tbsp. unsalted butter
1 potato, or 1 white turnip, peeled and cut into ¼-inch cubes
1 onion, chopped
1 garlic clove, finely chopped
¼ lb. mushrooms, wiped clean and quartered
1 small carrot, quartered lengthwise and cut into ¼-inch pieces
¼ tsp. salt
freshly ground black pepper
1 tbsp. flour
1 tbsp. chopped fresh sage, or ¾ tsp. dried sage
1 small zucchini, halved lengthwise and cut into ¼-inch slices
2 cups unsalted chicken stock
2 tbsp. cornstarch, mixed with 4 tbsp. white wine
Phyllo crust
1 cup flour
2 tbsp. virgin olive oil
¼ tsp. salt
3 tbsp. cornstarch
1 tbsp. unsalted butter

To prepare the pie filling, melt the butter in a large, heavy-bottomed saucepan over medium heat. Add the potato or turnip, and cook, stirring, for two minutes. Add the onion, garlic, mushrooms, carrot, salt and pepper. Stir in the flour and mix well. Cook for five minutes, stirring. Add the sage, zucchini and chicken pieces. Cook, stirring, until the zucchini is soft — about five minutes more.

Meanwhile, heat the chicken stock in a saucepan over medium-high heat and reduce it to about 1½ cups. Whisk the cornstarch mixture into the stock and simmer until the sauce is thickened and shiny — about two minutes. Pour this sauce into the chicken mixture, mix well, and set aside.

To prepare the phyllo crust, place the flour in a large bowl and make a well in the center. Pour the oil and salt into the well. Slowly stir in lukewarm water — up to ⅓ cup — until a soft dough results. On a board sprinkled with 1 tablespoon of the cornstarch, knead the dough until it is very elastic — at least 15 minutes. Dust a large work surface with the remaining 2 tablespoons of cornstarch and place the ball of dough in the center. Roll the dough into a uniformly thin circle.

Preheat the oven to 325° F. Melt the butter and brush half of it over the dough. Start pulling the dough gently but steadily in every direction until it forms a circle 2 to 2½ feet in diameter and nearly paper thin. Fold the dough in half, then fold it in half again to make a quarter circle. Over the dough, fit a round 10-inch baking dish or quiche pan that is at least 1½ inches deep. Cut the dough into a circle ½ inch larger than the pan all around.

Pour the filling into the ungreased baking dish. Fold the dough exactly in half to spread it over half of the filling and pan, then unfold it over the rest of the pie. Brush the top of the pie with the remaining 1½ teaspoons of melted butter. Put the pot pie in the oven and bake it until the surface of the dough turns golden — 20 to 25 minutes.

SUGGESTED ACCOMPANIMENT: *Bibb lettuce salad.*

EDITOR'S NOTE: *Three sheets of commercially prepared phyllo dough may be substituted for the handmade phyllo called for in this recipe.*

2 *Sliced for a party, a galantine made from a whole boned turkey reveals the colorful mosaic of its fresh vegetable stuffing (recipe, page 110).*

Turkey Transformed

Long a Thanksgiving and Christmas favorite, turkey has expanded far beyond its traditional culinary horizons. It is not only available year round today but can be bought fresh or frozen, in parts and even ground. As for cooking options, it can be sautéed, poached, stir fried, baked, stewed, broiled or braised, as well as stuffed and roasted. And there is no better meat from the viewpoint of nutritionists: A three-ounce serving of skinned breast, for example, contains even less saturated fat (only .2 grams) than skinned chicken, and it has fewer calories to boot. The growing popularity of turkey is reflected in the statistics: In 1960, per capita consumption was only 6.1 pounds; today it has almost doubled, and the numbers are continuing to rise.

The mild flavor and tenderness of the white meat make turkey breast a prime substitute for veal in some dishes, while the more richly flavored dark meat can serve as the base for other dishes normally made with lamb or pork. Yet turkey is never more interesting and exciting than when used in its own right as a "new" meat that invites fresh approaches.

The 26 recipes contained in this section demonstrate turkey's many possibilities both as family fare and as food that will surprise and please guests. Fresh, rather than frozen or cooked meat, is generally called for. Cutlets may be cut from whole and half breasts at home, a moneysaving measure that also allows the cook to determine the thickness of the slices or cutlets — but prepackaged cutlets can also be used. In most instances, the skin is removed; the phrase appearing in some of the recipes, "turkey breast meat," means not only raw and skinless, but boneless as well. One pound of turkey breast generally yields eight cutlets of about ¼-inch thickness. They can be pounded lightly to make them thinner; in the techniques section in the back of the book are instructions for slicing and pounding cutlets from the breast *(page 139),* and for boning a thigh *(page 138).*

Whatever the method of preparation, it is important to remember one thing: Like chicken, turkey is best when not overcooked. Only then will all the flavor and juiciness of the bird be present.

Turkey Patties with Beet Sauce

Serves 8
Working time: about 1 hour and 30 minutes
Total time: about 1 hour and 30 minutes

Calories **271**	1 lb. turkey meat, finely chopped
Protein **22g.**	1 tbsp. virgin olive oil
Cholesterol **46mg.**	2 cups finely shredded beet greens, mustard greens, Swiss chard or curly endive
Total fat **9g.**	4 garlic cloves, finely chopped
Saturated fat **4g.**	3 medium potatoes, peeled, boiled, mashed and chilled (about 2 cups)
Sodium **438mg.**	1½ cups part-skim ricotta cheese, drained in a strainer for ½ hour
	1 cup chopped scallions
	1 tbsp. grainy mustard
	¼ cup chopped fresh basil, or 2 tbsp. dried basil
	1 cup dry bread crumbs
	½ tsp. salt
	freshly ground black pepper

Beet sauce
2 tsp. unsalted butter
1 medium beet, peeled and julienned
¼ tsp. salt
1 cup unsalted turkey or chicken stock
1 tbsp. grainy mustard
¼ cup sliced scallions
½ tsp. arrowroot, or ½ tsp. cornstarch mixed with 1 tbsp. cold water

To make the patties, heat the olive oil in a sauté pan over medium heat. Add the greens and sprinkle the garlic on top. Reduce the heat to low, cover, and wilt the greens for about three minutes. Uncover, stir, and remove the pan from the heat. Allow to cool.

Preheat the oven to 375° F.

In a large bowl, mix together the turkey, mashed potatoes, ricotta cheese, scallions, mustard, basil, ½ cup of the bread crumbs and the cooled greens. Season with the salt and pepper. Form the mixture into 16 patties about 4 inches in diameter and ½ inch thick.

To make the sauce, melt the butter in a heavy-bottomed sauté pan over medium heat. Add the beet julienne and the salt and lightly sauté for five minutes. Add the stock and continue cooking over low heat until the sauce is reduced by one third and the beets are tender — about 10 minutes. Stir in the mustard, scallions, and arrowroot or cornstarch-and-water mixture, and continue to simmer until slightly thickened — about three minutes.

Dust the patties with the remaining ½ cup of bread crumbs. Place the patties on a nonstick baking sheet and bake until just lightly colored — 15 to 20 minutes.

To serve the patties, place them on a heated serving platter. Spoon the sauce over them.

SUGGESTED ACCOMPANIMENT: *fresh green-bean salad with sliced onions.*

Turkey Crust Pizza

Serves 8
Working time: about 30 minutes
Total time: about 1 hour and 30 minutes

Calories **291**
Protein **32g.**
Cholesterol **77mg.**
Total fat **11g.**
Saturated fat **4g.**
Sodium **461mg.**

2 lbs. white and dark turkey meat, skinned, ground or finely chopped
½ cup dry bread crumbs
1 scallion, chopped
2 egg whites, lightly beaten
4 drops hot red pepper sauce
2 tsp. virgin olive oil
¼ tsp. salt
freshly ground black pepper
2 tbsp. white wine
1¼ cups grated part-skim mozzarella and Gruyère cheese, combined
Pizza sauce
1 tbsp. virgin olive oil
½ cup finely chopped onion
1 large green or red pepper, halved, seeded, deribbed and cut into narrow strips
1½ cups thinly sliced mushrooms
35 oz. canned Italian whole plum tomatoes
2 large garlic cloves, finely chopped
2 tbsp. red wine vinegar
2 tsp. sugar
1 tbsp. chopped fresh basil, or 1 tsp. dried basil
½ tsp. dried oregano
¼ tsp. salt
freshly ground black pepper

To make the sauce, place the oil in a heavy-bottomed saucepan over medium-low heat, and cook the onion for three minutes, stirring frequently. Add the pepper strips and mushrooms and cook for two minutes. Add the rest of the sauce ingredients. Bring to a boil, reduce the heat and simmer gently for 40 minutes, stirring occasionally.

Preheat the oven to 400° F. Combine the bread crumbs, scallion, egg whites, hot red pepper sauce, 1 teaspoon of the oil, and the salt and pepper in a large bowl. Add ½ cup of the pizza sauce and the white wine. Mix in the ground turkey.

Rub a shallow 10- to 12-inch round baking dish with the remaining teaspoon of oil. Spread the turkey mixture evenly over the bottom of the dish, pushing it up all around the sides to resemble a crust. Pour half of the warm sauce onto the turkey crust. Cover with the grated cheeses. Ladle the remaining sauce over the cheese layer. Sprinkle with freshly ground black pepper. Place the dish on the upper level of the oven and bake for 15 minutes. Remove and let stand for five minutes. Cut in wedges and serve immediately.

SUGGESTED ACCOMPANIMENT: *romaine lettuce salad with garlic vinaigrette.*

Turkey Rolled with Ham and Mozzarella

THIS IS A LIVELY VARIATION ON VEAL CORDON BLEU.

Serves 6
Working time: about 30 minutes
Total time: about 40 minutes

Calories **256**
Protein **29g.**
Cholesterol **63mg.**
Total fat **11g.**
Saturated fat **4g.**
Sodium **517mg.**

eight ¼-inch-thick turkey cutlets (about 1 lb.), pounded to ⅛-inch thickness
4 oz. thinly sliced ham
5 oz. part-skim mozzarella, thinly sliced
freshly ground black pepper
3 tbsp. plain low-fat yogurt
⅓ cup dry bread crumbs
1 tbsp. virgin olive oil
fresh sage or parsley for garnish (optional)

Tomato sauce with sage
2 scallions, chopped
¼ cup dry white wine
1 medium tomato, peeled, seeded and finely chopped
1 tbsp. finely chopped fresh sage, or 1 tsp. dried sage
1 cup unsalted turkey or chicken stock
⅛ tsp. salt

Preheat the oven to 350° F. Lay out the turkey slices on a counter top, overlapping them to form a large rectangle. Cover the turkey with overlapping ham slices. Place the cheese on the ham; be sure to leave a ¾-inch border all around. Sprinkle with the pepper.

Roll the turkey tightly, starting from one of the long sides and using a spatula to nudge the meat over. Tuck in the ends to keep the cheese from leaking out during cooking.

Coat the turkey with the yogurt, then the bread crumbs. Place the roll in a large, shallow baking dish and dribble the olive oil over it. Bake the roll until firm and springy to the touch — about 20 minutes. Remove the roll from the oven and let it rest for five to seven minutes as the melted cheese firms up.

While the turkey is baking, prepare the sauce. Combine the scallions and white wine in a small saucepan and reduce the liquid to half, about 2 tablespoons. Add the tomato, sage, stock and salt and simmer for 10 minutes, stirring occasionally.

Cut the turkey into ⅓-inch slices. Arrange the slices on a heated serving dish, ladle on the hot sauce and garnish with fresh sage or parsley.

SUGGESTED ACCOMPANIMENT: *steamed spinach.*

Turkey Legs Baked with Yams and Apples

Serves 6
Working time: about 45 minutes
Total time: about 1 hour and 15 minutes

Calories **355**
Protein **30g.**
Cholesterol **104mg.**
Total fat **16g.**
Saturated fat **7g.**
Sodium **264mg.**

2 whole turkey legs, thigh bones removed
½ tsp. salt
freshly ground black pepper
2 tbsp. unsalted butter
¾ lb. yams, peeled and sliced into ¼-inch rounds
2 cups chopped scallions
2 tart green apples, peeled, cored and sliced into rings ¼ inch thick
1 tsp. fresh thyme, or ¼ tsp. dried thyme leaves
½ tsp. safflower oil
½ cup unsalted turkey or chicken stock

Preheat the oven to 450° F. Season the legs inside and out with the salt and pepper. Tie the boneless thighs with butcher's twine as for a roast.

Spread the bottom of a baking dish with the butter. Layer the yams, scallions and apples in the baking dish. Place the legs on top, sprinkle with the thyme, and rub with the safflower oil.

Bake at 450° F. for 20 minutes, then reduce the heat to 400° F. Pour the stock over the legs and cook until the juices run clear when a thigh is pierced with the tip of a sharp knife — about 25 minutes more. Remove the butcher's twine. Slice the thighs ¼ inch thick and cut the meat off the drumsticks. Arrange the meat on a heated platter with the yams and apples.

Turkey and Green-Chili Enchiladas

Serves 4
Working time: about 40 minutes
Total time: about 1 hour

Calories **456**
Protein **38g.**
Cholesterol **71mg.**
Total fat **16g.**
Saturated fat **4g.**
Sodium **377mg.**

2½ to 3 cups shredded or slivered cooked turkey meat (about ¾ lb.)
1 to 3 fresh hot green chilies, stemmed, seeded and finely chopped (see caution, page 25)
1 or 2 fresh jalapeño peppers, stemmed, seeded and coarsely chopped (see caution, page 25)
1 large onion, coarsely chopped
1 large tomato, cored, seeded and coarsely chopped
2 garlic cloves, coarsely chopped
2 tbsp. chopped cilantro
¼ cup unsalted turkey or chicken stock
2 tbsp. fresh lemon juice
⅛ tsp. sugar
¾ lb. tomatillos, papery husks removed, blanched 2 minutes, cored and quartered
1 cup grated Monterey Jack cheese (about 3 oz.)
½ tsp. ground cumin
1 tsp. chopped fresh oregano, or ¼ tsp. dried oregano
⅛ tsp. salt
8 corn tortillas
½ cup sour cream
½ cup plain low-fat yogurt

Preheat the oven to 350° F. Scrape half of the green chilies into a food processor or blender. Add the jalapeño peppers, onion, tomato, garlic, cilantro, stock, lemon juice and sugar. Using short bursts, process the mixture into a rough purée — about eight seconds. Add the tomatillos and process until coarsely chopped

— about five seconds. Pour the sauce into a saucepan and simmer it over medium heat for 10 minutes.

Next, make the filling for the tortillas. In a large bowl, combine the turkey, ⅔ cup of the cheese, the remaining green chilies, the cumin, oregano, salt and half of the sauce.

Place a heavy-bottomed skillet over medium heat. Warm a tortilla on the skillet for 10 seconds on each side to soften it, then place it in the hot sauce, carefully turn it over, and transfer it to a plate. Spoon about ⅓ cup of the turkey filling down the center of the tortilla, then roll it up to enclose the filling, and place it seam side down in a large oiled baking dish. Fill the remaining tortillas.

Pour the rest of the hot sauce over the enchiladas and sprinkle them with the remaining cheese. Bake, uncovered, for 20 minutes. Meanwhile, combine the sour cream and yogurt as a topping; spoon it over the enchiladas just before serving them.

SUGGESTED ACCOMPANIMENT: *curly endive salad.*
EDITOR'S NOTE: *The tomatillos called for in this recipe are also known as Mexican ground cherries. If tomatillos are unavailable, substitute ¾ pound of fresh green unripe tomatoes, coarsely chopped.*

Turkey Curry with Puréed Yams

Serves 6
Working time: about 30 minutes
Total time: about 1 hour and 45 minutes

Calories **336**
Protein **25g.**
Cholesterol **77mg.**
Total fat **12g.**
Saturated fat **6g.**
Sodium **253mg.**

1¼ lbs. boneless dark turkey meat, skinned and cut into 1-inch cubes
3 tbsp. unsalted butter
2 small yams, peeled and cut into ½-inch cubes
2 medium onions, finely chopped
1 celery stalk, finely chopped
2 garlic cloves, finely chopped
½ tsp. grated fresh ginger, or ¼ tsp. ground ginger
½ tsp. fresh thyme, or ⅛ tsp. dried thyme leaves
2 tbsp. curry powder
5 tbsp. fresh lemon juice
¼ tsp. salt
freshly ground black pepper
3 cups unsalted turkey or chicken stock
⅓ cup golden raisins
1 cup green peas

In a saucepan, bring 4 cups of water to a boil. Add the turkey cubes, blanch them for one minute, and drain.

In a large, heavy-bottomed skillet over low heat, melt half of the butter. Add the yams and cook them slowly, stirring frequently, until they are browned and tender — about 25 minutes. Purée the yams in a food processor or blender, and set them aside.

Over medium-low heat, melt the remaining 4½ teaspoons butter in the skillet. Add the onions, celery, garlic, ginger and thyme. Cook, stirring frequently, until the onions begin to brown — about 15 minutes.

Add the turkey, curry powder, lemon juice, salt and pepper. Reduce the heat to low and gently stir in the stock. Cover and simmer for 45 minutes. Uncover the skillet and add the raisins and the yam purée. Cover it again and cook, stirring occasionally, until the turkey is tender — about 30 minutes more. Add the peas and cook another five minutes. Serve immediately.

SUGGESTED ACCOMPANIMENTS: *steamed rice with cashews.*

Turkey Cutlets with Citrus

Serves 4
Working time: about 30 minutes
Total time: about 30 minutes

Calories **264**
Protein **27g.**
Cholesterol **66mg.**
Total fat **11g.**
Saturated fat **3g.**
Sodium **127mg.**

eight ¼-inch-thick turkey cutlets (about 1 lb.), pounded to ⅛-inch thickness
1 large navel orange
1 lime
flour for dredging
1 ½ tbsp. virgin olive oil
¼ cup dry white wine
¼ cup unsalted turkey or chicken stock
1 tbsp. finely chopped shallots, or 2 scallions, chopped
1 tsp. finely chopped fresh thyme, or ¼ tsp. dried thyme leaves
1 tsp. finely chopped fresh sage, or ¼ tsp. dried sage
½ tsp. sugar
⅛ tsp. salt
freshly ground black pepper
1 tbsp. unsalted butter
2 tbsp. coarsely chopped parsley

Use a knife to cut the peel from the orange and lime, taking care to remove all of the bitter white pith. Cut the fruit into ¼-inch cubes and set aside.

Make ⅛-inch slits along the cutlets' edges at 1- to 2-inch intervals to prevent the turkey from curling while cooking. Dredge the cutlets in the flour and shake off the excess. Heat a large heavy-bottomed skillet over medium-high heat and add 1 tablespoon of the oil. Put four cutlets in the pan and sauté for 45 seconds. Turn them over and sauté until the pink around the edges has turned white — about 30 seconds more. Transfer the cooked cutlets to a heated serving plate and keep warm. Add the remaining ½ tablespoon of oil to the pan, sauté the rest of the cutlets, and keep warm.

To prepare the sauce, add the wine, stock and shallots to the skillet and bring to a boil over medium-high heat. Reduce the liquid by half, to about ¼ cup, stirring frequently. Lower the heat to medium and stir in the fruit, thyme, sage, sugar, salt and pepper. Whisk in the butter and simmer, stirring occasionally, for five minutes. Add the parsley at the last minute. Pour the sauce over the cutlets and serve immediately.

SUGGESTED ACCOMPANIMENT: *bulgur; green peas.*

Minced Turkey with Lime and Cilantro

Serves 26-32 as a party snack, 8 as a main course
Working time: about 30 minutes
Total time: about 30 minutes

Calories **160**
Protein **16g.**
Cholesterol **31mg.**
Total fat **6g.**
Saturated fat **1g.**
Sodium **201mg.**

¾ lb. cooked turkey breast meat, finely chopped
Yogurt sauce
1 cup plain low-fat yogurt
1 tsp. finely chopped cilantro
1 tsp. sugar
2 tbsp. fresh lime juice
⅛ tsp. salt
⅛ tsp. cayenne pepper
Turkey morsels
½ cup fresh bread crumbs
⅓ cup finely sliced scallion greens
zest of 1 lime, grated
2 tsp. finely chopped cilantro
¼ tsp. chili powder
¼ tsp. salt
1 egg white
¼ cup flour
2 tbsp. safflower oil

To prepare the sauce, pour the yogurt into a small bowl and whisk in the cilantro, sugar, lime juice, salt and cayenne. Let stand 15 minutes.

Place the turkey in a bowl with the bread crumbs, scallions, zest, cilantro, chili powder and salt. Add the egg white and knead by hand or mix with a spoon.

With dampened hands, gently form the meat mixture into balls the size of large marbles and lightly dust with flour. Heat the oil in a heavy-bottomed skillet over medium heat and fry as many balls as possible without crowding until brown all over — for five or six minutes. Drain on paper towels and transfer to a warm platter. Serve with the sauce.

Chilled Turkey with Creamy Tuna Sauce

THIS RECIPE WAS INSPIRED BY VITELLO TONNATO,
THE CLASSIC ITALIAN VEAL DISH

Serves 6
Working time: about 30 minutes
Total time: about 40 minutes

Calories **287**
Protein **31g.**
Cholesterol **70mg.**
Total fat **15g.**
Saturated fat **2g.**
Sodium **125mg.**

1½ lb. boneless turkey breast meat, skinned and cut into ¾-by-1-inch chunks
½ tsp. virgin olive oil
½ tsp. safflower oil
⅛ tsp. salt
½ cup unsalted turkey or chicken stock, warmed
4 fresh sage leaves, finely sliced for garnish (optional)

Tuna sauce

one 3½ oz. can white tuna, packed in water, drained
3 tbsp. virgin olive oil
2 tbsp. safflower oil
5 tbsp. buttermilk
1 tsp. fresh lime juice
1 tsp. capers, rinsed and patted dry

Heat the oils in a large heavy-bottomed skillet over medium heat. Sauté the turkey pieces for three minutes and turn them over. Sprinkle with the salt and cook for another three minutes. Add the stock, lower the heat, and simmer for two minutes more. Remove each piece as it whitens. Set aside to cool. Reduce the stock to about ¼ cup and reserve for the sauce.

To make the sauce, purée the tuna with the stock in a food processor or a blender. Scrape down the sides with a rubber spatula and process another 10 seconds. With the motor still running, pour in the oils slowly. Add the buttermilk, lime juice and capers, and process for one minute more or until smooth. (If you lack either appliance, you may pound the tuna to a paste in a mortar.) Transfer the sauce to a bowl and refrigerate.

To assemble the dish, pour a little sauce on individual plates. Put a portion of the turkey on each plate and dribble the remaining sauce over the turkey. Garnish with the sage or with chopped parsley.

SUGGESTED ACCOMPANIMENT: *julienned carrots; Italian bread.*

Turkey Scallops with Pine Nuts and Currants

Serves: 4
Working time: about 50 minutes
Total time: about 50 minutes

Calories **451**
Protein **33g.**
Cholesterol **59mg.**
Total fat **26g.**
Saturated fat **4g.**
Sodium **485mg.**

eight ¼-inch turkey breast cutlets (about 1 lb.), pounded to ⅛ inch thickness
3 egg whites
½ tsp. salt
freshly ground black pepper
3 tbsp. virgin olive oil
2 to 3 tbsp. finely chopped shallots
⅓ cup white wine vinegar
10 whole black peppercorns
3 bay leaves
3 tbsp. currants
⅓ cup safflower oil
⅔ cup dry bread crumbs
½ cup finely chopped fresh parsley
2 garlic cloves, finely chopped
zest of ½ orange, finely chopped or grated
3 tbsp. pine nuts, lightly toasted

In a shallow bowl, beat the egg whites with the salt and pepper. Add the cutlets one at a time, turning them to coat them with the mixture.

In a small heavy-bottomed saucepan, heat the olive oil. Add the shallots and sauté over medium heat until translucent — about five minutes. Add the vinegar, water, peppercorns and bay leaves, and simmer for 20 minutes. Stir in the currants and simmer for another 10 minutes, or until the liquid is reduced by half, to about ½ cup.

In the meantime, heat the safflower oil in a large heavy-bottomed skillet. Spread the bread crumbs in a plate. Dip the cutlets in the crumbs, then brown them in the hot oil over medium to high heat for one to two minutes on each side. Put the cooked cutlets on a heated platter and cover with foil to keep warm.

To assemble, combine the parsley, garlic and zest. Strain the reduced sauce, reserving the currants, and pour it evenly over the turkey cutlets. Sprinkle with the currants, the parsley mixture and the pine nuts. Serve warm or, if preferred, at room temperature.

SUGGESTED ACCOMPANIMENTS: *risotto; broccoli salad with julienned red pepper.*

Turkey-Stuffed Pitas

Serves 8
Working time: about 45 minutes
Total time: about 1 hour and 30 minutes

Calories **368**
Protein **27g.**
Cholesterol **44mg.**
Total fat **14g.**
Saturated fat **2g.**
Sodium **136mg.**

1½ lb. turkey breast meat, skinned
2 tsp. safflower oil
juice of 1 lime
8 small whole-wheat pitas (pocket bread)
1½ cups shredded lettuce

Dry marinade

1 tbsp. paprika
2 tbsp. finely chopped onion
2 garlic cloves, finely chopped
¼ tsp. cayenne pepper
¼ tsp. white pepper
½ tsp. crushed fennel seeds
2 tsp. fresh thyme, or ½ tsp. dried thyme leaves
½ tsp. dried oregano

Vegetable filling

1 large avocado, peeled and cut into ¼-inch cubes
juice of ½ lemon
2 large tomatoes, halved, seeded and coarsely chopped
⅔ cup finely chopped onion
1 large green pepper, seeded, deribbed and cut into ¼-inch pieces

Yogurt dressing

3 tbsp. fresh lime juice
1 tbsp. red wine vinegar
5 drops hot red pepper sauce
1 tbsp. honey
2 tsp. Dijon mustard
2 garlic cloves, finely chopped
2 tbsp. chopped cilantro
¼ tsp. salt
2 tbsp. safflower oil
½ cup plain low-fat yogurt

In a small bowl, combine the marinade ingredients.

Use a sharp knife to crisscross both sides of the turkey with ⅓-inch deep cuts, ¾ of an inch apart. Rub in the marinade, making sure the seasonings fill the cuts, and refrigerate for one hour.

While the turkey is marinating, prepare the vegetable filling. In a bowl, sprinkle the avocado with the lemon juice and toss to keep it from turning brown. Combine with the tomato, onion and green pepper. Refrigerate until ready to serve.

Preheat the oven to 400° F. To prepare the dressing, combine the lime juice, vinegar, hot red pepper sauce, honey, mustard, garlic, cilantro and salt in a large bowl, and whisk vigorously. Whisk in the oil slowly. Then whisk in the yogurt and refrigerate.

In a large heavy-bottomed ovenproof skillet, heat the 2 teaspoons of safflower oil over medium-high heat. Sauté the turkey on one side until brown — about five minutes. Turn, cook for one minute, then place the skillet in the upper level of the oven. Roast the turkey until the flesh is firm and springy to the

touch — eight to 12 minutes. Remove from the skillet, squeeze the lime juice over the meat, and allow to stand for five minutes. Slice against the grain into ¼-inch-thick pieces. Cut each into strips.

To assemble the pitas, place them in the hot oven for one minute to soften. Slice each open at the top, stuff some shredded lettuce inside and fill the rest of the pocket with the turkey and the vegetable mixture. Serve the yogurt dressing separately.

Turkey Scallopini with Red and Green Peppers

Serves 4
Working time: about 15 minutes
Total time: about 30 minutes

Calories **237**
Protein **27g.**
Cholesterol **59mg.**
Total fat **11g.**
Saturated fat **2g.**
Sodium **207mg.**

eight ¼-inch-thick turkey cutlets (about 1 lb.), pounded to ⅛-inch thickness
½ cup flour
2 tbsp. safflower oil
1 tsp. virgin olive oil
¼ cup finely chopped onion
2 garlic cloves, finely chopped
¾ cup unsalted turkey or chicken stock
2 tbsp. chopped fresh basil, or 2 tsp. dried basil
2 tbsp. balsamic vinegar, or 1 tbsp. red wine vinegar
¼ tsp. salt
freshly ground black pepper
1 large green pepper, julienned
1 large red pepper, julienned

To prevent the turkey from curling while cooking, score the edges of the cutlets with ⅛-inch slits at 1- to 2-inch intervals. Dredge the cutlets in the flour and shake off the excess.

Heat a large, heavy-bottomed skillet over medium-high heat and add 1 tablespoon of the safflower oil. ▶

Put four cutlets in the pan and sauté them for 45 seconds. Turn them over and sauté them until their edges turn from pink to white — about 30 seconds more. Transfer the cooked cutlets to a heated platter. Add the remaining tablespoon of safflower oil to the skillet and sauté the other four cutlets. Remove the skillet from the heat and transfer the turkey to the platter. Cover loosely with foil and keep warm.

To prepare the peppers, reduce the heat to medium low and heat the olive oil in the skillet. Add the onion and garlic and cook until the onion is translucent — about 10 minutes. Then add the stock, basil, vinegar, salt, pepper and julienned peppers. Increase the heat to medium and simmer until the peppers are tender — about five minutes. Spoon the pepper mixture over the cutlets and serve the dish immediately.

SUGGESTED ACCOMPANIMENT: *spaghetti tossed with garlic and olive oil.*

Stir-Fried Turkey with Mixed Vegetables

Serves 4
Working time: about 30 minutes
Total time: about 40 minutes

Calories **211**
Protein **24g.**
Cholesterol **44mg.**
Total fat **10g.**
Saturated fat **2g.**
Sodium **350mg.**

¾ lb. turkey breast meat, cut into 2½-by-½-by-¼-inch strips
4 tsp. safflower oil or peanut oil
1 small red pepper, seeded, deribbed and cut into ¼-inch-wide strips
1 cup broccoli florets (about ½ lb.)
½ cup thinly sliced mushrooms
¼ cup snow peas, with strings removed
4 scallions, trimmed and coarsely chopped
1 cup sliced Nappa (Chinese) cabbage

Marinade

1 tsp. dark sesame oil
2 tbsp. low-sodium soy sauce
2 tbsp. finely chopped fresh ginger
2 garlic cloves, finely chopped

Sesame sauce

½ cup unsalted turkey or chicken stock
4 tsp. low-sodium soy sauce
1 tbsp. red wine vinegar
1 tbsp. sesame seeds
1 tsp. dark sesame oil
freshly ground black pepper

To prepare the marinade, combine the sesame oil, soy sauce, ginger and garlic. Add the turkey strips, toss, and set them aside to marinate for half an hour.

To make the sesame sauce, mix the stock, soy sauce, vinegar, sesame seeds, sesame oil and pepper in a small bowl, and set it aside.

Place a wok or heavy-bottomed skillet over high heat and add 2 teaspoons of the oil. When the oil is hot but not smoking, add the turkey strips and stir fry them, turning them with a metal spatula or slotted spoon, just until the meat turns white — about two minutes. Remove the wok or skillet from the heat and use a slotted spoon to transfer the turkey to a plate.

Heat the remaining 2 teaspoons of oil in the wok or skillet. Add the red pepper, broccoli, mushrooms and snow peas, and stir fry them for one minute. Add the scallions and cabbage, and cook the vegetables one minute more, stirring and tossing rapidly. Pour in the sauce and cook the mixture an additional two minutes, stirring constantly. Stir in the turkey and heat it through. Serve hot.

SUGGESTED ACCOMPANIMENT: *steamed rice.*
EDITOR'S NOTE: *Stir frying is designed to sear meats and cook vegetables quickly, without sacrificing their color, texture or flavor. It must be executed speedily so the meats will not toughen and the vegetables will not wilt.*

Turkey Satays with Peanut Sauce

SATAY IS AN INDONESIAN WORD FOR SKEWERED TIDBITS OF BROILED MEAT.

Serves 8
Working time: about 30 minutes
Total time: about 6 hours and 15 minutes

Calories **233**
Protein **29g.**
Cholesterol **59mg.**
Total fat **10g.**
Saturated fat **2g.**
Sodium **287mg.**

2 lbs. turkey breast meat, skinned and cut into 1-inch cubes
Marinade
1 cup plain low-fat yogurt
¼ cup safflower oil
1 tbsp. grated fresh ginger
½ tsp. ground cardamom
½ tsp. ground coriander
¼ tsp. salt
½ tsp. freshly ground black pepper
2 tsp. paprika
Peanut sauce
⅓ cup peanut butter
1 cup boiling water
2 garlic cloves, finely chopped
2 tbsp. fresh lemon juice
2 tbsp. low-sodium soy sauce
¼ tsp. crushed red pepper
2 tbsp. molasses

Whisk the marinade ingredients together. Add the cubed turkey and refrigerate for six hours or overnight, stirring occasionally to keep the pieces well coated.

If you plan to grill the turkey, light the coals about 30 minutes before cooking time; for broiling, preheat the broiler with its rack and pan in place about 10 minutes beforehand.

To make the peanut sauce, first heat the peanut butter in a heavy-bottomed saucepan over low heat. Whisk in the boiling water, then stir in the garlic, lemon juice, soy sauce, red pepper and molasses. Bring the mixture to a boil and whisk it until it thickens — about two minutes. Taste the sauce and add more red pepper or molasses if desired. Pour into a sauceboat.

Thread the turkey cubes onto skewers, preferably square or flat-bladed, so the cubes will not slip when turned and cook unevenly. Grill the cubes over the hot coals, turning them several times, for about eight minutes. Broiling may take as long as 15 minutes — about four minutes for each side. To test for doneness, make a small cut in a turkey cube to see whether its center has turned from pink to white. Arrange the satays on a heated platter and serve the sauce separately.

SUGGESTED ACCOMPANIMENT: *fried rice.*

boiling water for one minute, drain and refresh under cold water. Put the parsley in a food processor or blender, add the reduced poaching liquid, and purée. Keep warm.

In a heavy-bottomed skillet, cook the leek in 1 tablespoon butter over low heat until soft — about 10 minutes. Transfer to a plate. Cook the radishes in the remaining 1 tablespoon butter for one minute.

To assemble, slice the turkey rolls thinly on the diagonal and arrange in an attractive pattern on individual plates. Decorate with the leeks and radishes, and pour a little sauce on each plate, taking care not to cover the meat or vegetables.

SUGGESTED ACCOMPANIMENT: *braised fennel.*

Turkey Rolls with Parsley Sauce

Serves 4
Working time: about 1 hour
Total time: about 1 hour

Calories **365**
Protein **44g.**
Cholesterol **179mg.**
Total fat **14g.**
Saturated fat **6g.**
Sodium **456mg.**

eight ¼-inch-thick turkey breast cutlets (about 1 lb.), pounded to ⅛ inch thickness
½ lb. skinned, finely chopped turkey leg meat
2 egg whites, plus 1 whole egg
¼ cup finely chopped fresh parsley, plus 2 cups parsley leaves
½ tsp. salt
freshly ground black pepper
2 cups unsalted turkey or chicken stock
½ cup dry white wine
1 medium-size leek, cut into 3-inch-long sections, finely sliced along their length
2 tbsp. unsalted butter
8 radishes, thinly sliced

In a food processor or blender, combine the chopped turkey leg meat with the egg whites and the whole egg, and process until smooth. Transfer the mixture to a bowl; add the chopped parsley, salt and pepper, mixing well. Put an eighth of this stuffing on the center of each cutlet, wrap the sides of the cutlet around it and secure with wooden picks.

Place the turkey rolls in a large shallow sauté pan. Add the stock and wine. Bring the liquid to a boil, reduce the heat and simmer, covered, until tender — about 20 minutes. With a slotted spoon, transfer the rolls to a heated plate and cover with foil to keep warm. Reduce the poaching liquid to about ¾ cup.

Meanwhile, blanch the 2 cups of parsley leaves in

Rolled Turkey Cutlets Stuffed with Buckwheat

Serves 6
Working time: about 45 minutes
Total time: about 45 minutes

Calories **243**
Protein **24g.**
Cholesterol **46mg.**
Total fat **8g.**
Saturated fat **2g.**
Sodium **343mg.**

eight ¼-inch-thick turkey breast cutlets (about 1 lb.), pounded to ⅛-inch thickness
¾ lb. fresh spinach, stemmed and washed
Buckwheat stuffing
1 tbsp. unsalted butter
1 medium onion, finely chopped
1 small celery stalk, diced
½ cup roasted buckwheat groats (kasha), preferably whole kernels
¼ cup dry white wine
1¼ cups thinly sliced fresh mushrooms
2 garlic cloves, finely chopped
1 tsp. fresh thyme, or ¼ tsp. dried thyme leaves
1 tbsp. virgin olive oil
1 cup unsalted turkey or chicken stock
½ tsp. salt
freshly ground black pepper
¼ cup wheat germ
1 egg white, lightly beaten
Madeira sauce
½ cup Madeira or medium-dry sherry
1 tbsp. finely chopped shallot
1 tsp. fresh thyme, or ¼ tsp. dried thyme leaves
1 cup unsalted turkey or chicken stock
2 tbsp. balsamic vinegar, or 1 tbsp. red wine vinegar
⅛ tsp. salt

Blanch the spinach for one minute and refresh with cold water. Squeeze out the water and set aside.

To make the stuffing, melt the butter in a heavy-bottomed saucepan over medium-low heat, and cook the onion and celery until the onion is translucent — about 10 minutes. Stir in the buckwheat groats and cook for one minute. Add the wine, mushrooms, garlic, thyme, oil, stock, salt and pepper. Bring to a simmer, reduce the heat, and cover. Cook until the liquid is absorbed — 10 to 15 minutes. Off the heat, stir in the wheat germ. Add the beaten egg white and blend thoroughly. Set aside to cool.

Lay the cutlets on a flat surface and cover them with the spinach leaves. Place 3 tablespoons of the stuffing on each cutlet and roll up tightly. Sprinkle with pepper. Wrap each roll in plastic wrap, then wrap again to make the packages watertight. Pour enough water into a large, deep skillet or pot to fill it 2 inches deep. Bring the water to a boil and add the rolls. Reduce the heat and simmer, turning the rolls after 10 minutes, until no pink meat is visible — about 20 minutes in all.

To make the sauce, put the Madeira, the shallot and the thyme in a small saucepan. Bring to a boil, then lower the heat and reduce the liquid by half. Add the stock, vinegar and salt, and bring back to a boil. Reduce the heat again and simmer for 10 minutes.

To serve, remove the plastic wrap from the turkey and slice each roll diagonally into ½-inch pieces. Arrange the slices on a warmed serving platter and spoon the sauce over them.

SUGGESTED ACCOMPANIMENT: *steamed Savoy cabbage*.

Turkey Salad with Yogurt and Buttermilk Dressing

Serves 6
Working time: about 30 minutes
Total time: about 30 minutes

Calories **331**
Protein **27g.**
Cholesterol **53mg.**
Total fat **14g.**
Saturated fat **3g.**
Sodium **213mg.**

2¼ cups cooked turkey breast meat, skinned and cut into ½-inch cubes (about 1 lb.)
1¼ lb. small new potatoes
2 tbsp. virgin olive oil
1 cup medium mushrooms, quartered
⅛ tsp. salt
1 large green pepper, seeded, deribbed and cut into ½-inch chunks
2 tbsp. dry white wine
½ cup watercress leaves
½ cup chopped scallions
1 head Bibb lettuce, washed and trimmed
2 medium tomatoes
1 small cucumber, sliced
1 medium red onion, thinly sliced
Yogurt and buttermilk dressing
1 scallion, chopped
2 tbsp. red wine vinegar
1 tbsp. fresh lemon juice
½ tsp. celery seed
4 drops hot red pepper sauce
¼ tsp. salt
freshly ground black pepper
3 tbsp. virgin olive oil
¼ cup buttermilk
¼ cup plain low-fat yogurt
1 garlic clove, chopped

Turkey Salad with Feta Cheese

Serves 4
Working time: about 20 minutes
Total time: about 20 minutes

Calories **497**
Protein **42g.**
Cholesterol **103mg.**
Total fat **33g.**
Saturated fat **8g.**
Sodium **708mg.**

2¼ cups cooked turkey breast meat (about 1 lb.), skinned and cut into ½-inch cubes
1 small cucumber, peeled, halved, seeded and thinly cut on the diagonal
8 red radishes, diced
8 large Greek black olives, pitted and halved
4 oz. feta cheese, cut into cubes
1 lb. fresh spinach, stemmed, washed and dried
Basil vinaigrette
2 garlic cloves, finely chopped
2 tbsp. chopped fresh basil, or 2 tsp. dried basil
½ tsp. sugar
1 tbsp. grainy mustard
freshly ground black pepper
2 tbsp. fresh lemon juice
2 tbsp. red wine vinegar
2 tbsp. safflower oil
¼ cup virgin olive oil

To prepare the vinaigrette, place all the ingredients in a screw-top jar with a tight-fitting lid and shake vigorously until thoroughly blended — about 30 seconds.

To assemble the salad, combine the turkey, cucumber, radishes, olives and cheese in a large bowl, add the dressing, and toss. Arrange the spinach on salad plates and spoon the salad on top.

Drop the potatoes into boiling water, cover, and cook until tender, about 20 minutes. Drain. When they are cool enough to handle, cut the unskinned potatoes into ¾-inch cubes. Set aside in a warm place.

Heat the 2 tablespoons of olive oil in a small heavy-bottomed saucepan over medium heat. Add the mushrooms and the salt and cook for about one minute. Add the green pepper and the wine and continue cooking for five minutes, stirring occasionally.

Meanwhile, in a large bowl, combine the turkey, warm potatoes, watercress and scallions. Toss in the mushroom-and-pepper mixture. Set aside.

To prepare the dressing, place all the ingredients in a screw-top jar with a tight-fitting lid and shake vigorously until thoroughly blended, about 30 seconds.

Add the dressing to the turkey mixture and toss lightly. Arrange lettuce on individual plates and place a generous portion of the salad on each. Garnish with slices of tomato, cucumber and red onion.

Turkey and Black Bean Salad

Serves 10
Working time: about 30 minutes
Total time: about 1 day

Calories **393**
Protein **30g.**
Cholesterol **47mg.**
Total fat **16g.**
Saturated fat **2g.**
Sodium **260mg.**

3½ cups cooked turkey breast meat (about 1½ lb.), cut into thin strips
1⅔ cups dried black beans, soaked for 8 hours and drained
1 medium onion, coarsely chopped
2 garlic cloves, chopped
3-inch cinnamon stick, broken in half
1½ tsp. fresh thyme or ½ tsp. dried thyme leaves
1 small dried hot red chili pepper with seeds removed (see caution, page 25), or ¼ tsp. cayenne pepper
1 bay leaf
½ tsp. salt
½ lb. snow peas, with strings removed, sliced into thin strips
1 small cantaloupe, halved, seeded, and the flesh cut into small chunks
6 scallions, trimmed and finely sliced
3 medium tomatoes, peeled, seeded and coarsely chopped, placed in a strainer to drain
1 small green pepper, seeded, deribbed and chopped
1 head Bibb or red leaf lettuce
Cilantro dressing
¾ cup red wine vinegar
juice of 1 lemon or lime
2 tbsp. Dijon mustard
2 tbsp. honey
10 to 15 drops hot red pepper sauce
¼ tsp. salt
freshly ground black pepper
2 garlic cloves, chopped
5 tbsp. chopped cilantro
⅓ cup safflower oil
¼ cup virgin olive oil

Drain the soaked beans and put them into a heavy 4-quart casserole with the onion, garlic, cinnamon, thyme, chili pepper, bay leaf and salt. Add water to cover by 2 inches, bring to a boil, and boil for 10 minutes. Lower the heat and skim off the foam. Cover and simmer just until the beans are tender — one to one and a half hours. Drain the beans in a colander and rinse with cold water. Remove the chili pepper, cinnamon and bay leaf and allow the beans to drain further. (The beans can be prepared a day ahead.)

Blanch the snow peas in boiling water for 15 seconds and refresh them in cold water. Drain and place on paper towels to dry.

Put all the dressing ingredients, except the oils, in a food processor or blender and process for 15 seconds. Add the oil slowly and process until smooth, about 30 seconds more.

In a large bowl, combine the cantaloupe, scallions, tomatoes, green pepper and turkey. Add the snow peas and beans. Pour 1 cup of the dressing over the salad and toss lightly. To serve, mound the salad on lettuce leaves arranged on a platter or on individual plates and pass the remaining dressing.

Roast Breast of Turkey with Fruit Stuffing

Serves 8
Working time: about 30 minutes
Total time: about 1 hour

Calories **255**
Protein **23g.**
Cholesterol **59mg.**
Total fat **7g.**
Saturated fat **3g.**
Sodium **92mg.**

1¾ to 2 lb. boneless turkey breast half, with skin
⅛ tsp. salt
1 tbsp. safflower oil
chopped fresh sage or parsley for garnish

Fruit stuffing

2 tbsp. unsalted butter
⅓ cup finely chopped onion
1 large tart green apple, peeled, cored and diced
1 tsp. sugar
1 tsp. chopped fresh sage, or ¼ tsp. dried sage
¼ tsp. ground cloves
4 oz. dried apricots, cut into small pieces

⅓ cup seedless raisins
3 tbsp. unsalted turkey or chicken stock
¼ cup apple cider

Cider sauce

1 tbsp. finely chopped onion
2 tbsp. dry white wine
1 cup apple cider
½ cup unsalted turkey or chicken stock
1 tsp. red wine vinegar

To make the stuffing, melt the butter in a heavy-bottomed saucepan over medium heat. Sauté the onion until it is translucent — about 10 minutes. Add the apple and sugar and continue cooking, stirring occasionally, until the apple is tender but not mushy — about five minutes. Stir in the sage, cloves, apricots, raisins, stock and apple cider. Reduce the heat and cover the pan tightly. Cook until all of the liquid is absorbed — about five minutes — stirring once. Trans-

fer to a bowl and allow to cool. (The stuffing can be prepared a day ahead and refrigerated.)

Preheat the oven to 350° F. Put the turkey, skin side down, on a flat surface. Using a sharp knife, cut a flap in the breast by slicing from the long, thin side toward the thicker side, being careful not to cut all the way through. Open the flap and place the turkey between two pieces of plastic wrap. Pound lightly to flatten to an even thickness of about ½ inch. Sprinkle the turkey with the salt and mound the stuffing in the center. Wrap the flap around the stuffing and roll the breast snugly to form a cylinder with the skin on the outside. Tuck in the ends and tie securely with butcher's twine.

Heat the oil in a roasting pan and brown the skin side of the roll for three to four minutes. Turn the turkey skin side up and put the pan in the oven. Roast for 20 to 25 minutes, or until the juices run clear when the meat is pierced with the tip of a sharp knife. Remove the turkey from the pan and keep warm.

To make the sauce, pour off any fat in the pan and discard. Add the onion and wine and cook over medium-high heat, stirring to deglaze the pan. Add the cider, stock and vinegar and continue cooking until the sauce is reduced by a quarter — about 10 minutes.

To serve, remove the butcher's twine and cut the turkey into ¾-inch slices. Arrange on a heated serving platter and garnish with fresh sage leaves or parsley. Pass the sauce separately.

SUGGESTED ACCOMPANIMENT: *green peas and pearl onions.*

Roast Gingered Turkey Breast

Serves 6
Working time: about 10 minutes
Total time: about 1 day

Calories **162**
Protein **26g.**
Cholesterol **59mg.**
Total fat **5g.**
Saturated fat **1g.**
Sodium **164mg.**

1 turkey breast half (about 1½ lb.), skinned and boned
2 tsp. safflower oil
Ginger marinade
3 garlic cloves, finely chopped
¾ tsp. ground cinnamon
2 tbsp. peeled and grated fresh ginger
¼ cup unsalted turkey or chicken stock
1 tsp. dark sesame oil
1 tbsp. low-sodium soy sauce

To make the marinade, combine the garlic, cinnamon, ginger, stock, sesame oil and soy sauce in a shallow bowl just large enough to hold the turkey breast. Using a knife with a sharp point, poke several ½-inch-deep slits in the thick part of the meat to allow the marinade to penetrate. Put the turkey in the bowl with the marinade and turn it to coat it. Cover and refrigerate for eight to 24 hours, turning occasionally.

Preheat the oven to 350° F. Remove the turkey from the marinade, scraping any clinging garlic and ginger back into the bowl. Reserve the marinade and allow the turkey to come to room temperature. Heat the safflower oil in a heavy-bottomed ovenproof skillet over medium-high heat. Sauté the turkey until golden on one side — about four minutes — and turn. Use a pastry brush to baste with the accumulated juices and continue cooking for one minute. Put the skillet in the oven and roast the turkey until it feels firm but springy to the touch — 15 to 20 minutes — basting once with the reserved marinade. Let the turkey rest for at least five minutes before slicing. Serve hot or cold.

SUGGESTED ACCOMPANIMENTS: *rice salad with currants and toasted pine nuts; sautéed carrots.*

Honey-Glazed Roast Turkey

Serves 12
Working time: about 1 hour
Total time: about 5 hours

Calories **480**
Protein **50g.**
Cholesterol **151mg.**
Total fat **15g.**
Saturated fat **6g.**
Sodium **368mg.**

one 12 lb. fresh or thawed turkey, the neck, gizzard and heart reserved for gravy
¾ tsp. salt
freshly ground black pepper
2 tbsp. honey

Orange-and-sweet-potato stuffing

zest of 1 lemon, cut into fine strips
4 navel oranges, the zest of 2 cut into fine strips
6 medium sweet potatoes, peeled and cut into ½-inch cubes
6 tbsp. unsalted butter
3 large onions, chopped
¼ cup fresh lemon juice
½ cup unsalted turkey or chicken stock
⅛ tsp. salt
freshly ground black pepper
½ tsp. ground cloves
¾ tsp. dry mustard
6 slices cracked-wheat bread, cut into cubes and lightly toasted
2 tbsp. brandy

Port-and-orange gravy

the turkey neck, gizzard and heart
1 tbsp. safflower oil
1 carrot, chopped
1 celery stalk, coarsely chopped
2 medium onions, coarsely chopped
1 garlic clove, coarsely chopped
1 cup white wine
1 bay leaf
1 tsp. fresh thyme, or ¼ tsp. dried thyme leaves
the roasting juices from the turkey (about 1 cup), degreased
the juice and grated zest of one orange
1 tbsp. red wine vinegar
2 tbsp. cornstarch
⅓ cup port
½ tsp. salt
freshly ground black pepper

To prepare the stuffing, blanch the lemon and orange zest in 1 cup of boiling water for one minute. Drain and set aside. Using a sharp knife, peel the oranges and divide them into sections. Cut each section in half and reserve.

In a large saucepan, bring 2 quarts of water to a boil. Drop in the sweet-potato cubes and blanch them for three minutes. Drain and set aside.

In a large, heavy-bottomed casserole, melt 4 tablespoons of the butter over medium-low heat. Add the onion and cook it until translucent, stirring occasionally — about 10 minutes. Add the lemon and orange zest, oranges, sweet potatoes, lemon juice, stock, salt and pepper. Cook until the sweet potato cubes are tender — seven to 10 minutes. Remove from the heat and add the cloves, mustard, the remaining 2 tablespoons of butter, the bread cubes and the brandy. Mix thoroughly. Allow to cool before using.

To make a stock for the gravy, chop the turkey neck into pieces. Heat the oil in a heavy-bottomed saucepan over medium-high heat. Add the neck, gizzard, heart, carrot, celery, onions and garlic. Sauté, stirring, until the vegetables begin to brown — about five minutes. Add the white wine, bay leaf, thyme and 3 cups of water. Reduce the heat to low and simmer for one hour, skimming off impurities as necessary. Strain the stock, pushing down on the contents to extract all the liquid; there should be 2 to 2½ cups. Set it aside.

Preheat the oven to 350° F. Rinse the turkey inside and out under cold running water and dry it thoroughly with paper towels. Rub the salt and pepper inside the body and neck cavities and outside the bird.

To stuff the turkey, loosely fill both cavities. Tie the drumsticks together with butcher's twine and tuck the wing tips under the bird. Put the turkey on a rack in a shallow roasting pan. Add 1 cup of water to the pan.

To keep the turkey moist and prevent it from overbrowning, make a tent of aluminum foil. Use an extra-wide sheet of foil (or two sheets of regular foil crimped together) that measure 1½ feet longer than the pan. Lay the foil shiny side down over the turkey, and tuck it loosely around the inside edges of the pan. Roast the turkey in the oven for two and one half hours.

Take the turkey from the oven and carefully remove the foil tent. Brush the turkey all over with the honey. Turn the heat down to 325° F., then return the turkey to the oven, and roast it uncovered for one hour. The bird is done when a meat thermometer inserted in the thickest part of the thigh reads 180° F. There should be about 1 cup of roasting juices in the pan.

Let the turkey stand for at least 20 minutes before carving it. In the meantime, remove the stuffing from the cavities and set it aside in a bowl loosely covered with foil to keep it warm.

To make the gravy, combine the stock, reserved roasting juices, orange juice and zest, and vinegar in a saucepan. Bring the mixture to a boil. Mix the cornstarch and the port and whisk them into the saucepan; return the gravy to a boil. Reduce the heat to low and simmer for five minutes. Add the salt and pepper and serve piping hot with the carved bird and the stuffing.

EDITOR'S NOTE: *To roast a larger turkey, increase the cooking time by 20 to 25 minutes per pound, and leave the foil tent on until one hour of cooking time remains. To cook the turkey* unstuffed, rub orange peel and ¼ teaspoon of cloves inside the cavity for extra flavor, and subtract five minutes per pound from the total cooking time.

If you wish to cook the stuffing separately as a dressing, put it in a baking dish with an additional ¼ cup of stock. Cover the dish with aluminum foil and bake the dressing in a preheated 325° F. oven for 45 minutes. Uncover the dish and return it to the oven for another 45 minutes.

Buckwheat Stuffing

Serves 10
Enough for a 10-to-12-pound turkey
Working time: about 30 minutes
Total time: about 1 hour and 30 minutes

Calories **213**
Protein **7g.**
Cholesterol **10mg.**
Total fat **12g.**
Saturated fat **3g.**
Sodium **188mg.**

1 ½ cups toasted buckwheat groats (kasha)
3 tbsp. unsalted butter
½ lb. mushrooms, wiped clean and thinly sliced
1 celery stalk, finely chopped
2 cups chopped onions
3 garlic cloves, finely chopped
2 ½ cups unsalted turkey or chicken stock
½ cup port or dry sherry
½ tsp. salt
freshly ground black pepper
2 egg whites
1 ½ tsp. ground cinnamon
1 cup blanched almonds, toasted in a preheated 350° F. oven until lightly browned, then coarsely chopped
2 cups fresh parsley leaves

Melt 1 tablespoon of the butter in a large, heavy-bottomed skillet over medium-high heat. Sauté the mushrooms until they begin to brown — about seven minutes. Stir in the celery, onions and garlic. Reduce the heat to medium low, cover, and cook for three minutes. Uncover and continue cooking, stirring occasionally, until the onions are translucent — about five minutes more. Set the mixture aside.

In a saucepan, bring the stock, port or sherry, salt and pepper to a simmer. While the stock simmers, beat the egg whites in a mixing bowl. Add the buckwheat groats and stir until the grains are well coated.

In a large, heavy-bottomed casserole, melt the remaining 2 tablespoons of butter over medium-high heat. Add the coated buckwheat groats and stir constantly with a fork until the grains are dry and do not stick together — about two minutes. Pour in the simmering stock, then stir in the onion-and-mushroom mixture and the cinnamon. Reduce the heat to low, cover, and simmer until the grains are soft — about 15 minutes. Remove the mixture from the heat, add the almonds and parsley, and blend well with a fork.

Roast the bird until only one hour of cooking time remains. Remove it from the oven and pour the juices and fat from the breast cavity. Stuff the cavity with the buckwheat mixture, and finish roasting the turkey.

EDITOR'S NOTE: *If you wish to cook the stuffing separately as a dressing, put it in a baking dish and cover the dish with aluminum foil. Bake the dressing in a preheated 325° F. oven for 20 minutes. Uncover the baking dish, add ½ cup of stock, and return the dressing to the oven for another 20 minutes. If you roast a turkey without stuffing, put celery leaves, onion trimmings, parsley stems and a few garlic cloves in the breast cavity for extra flavor.*

Spinach, Beet-Green and Pine-Nut Stuffing

Serves 10
Enough for a 10-to-12-pound turkey
Working time: about 30 minutes
Total time: about 30 minutes

Calories **266**
Protein **11g.**
Cholesterol **7mg.**
Total fat **8g.**
Saturated fat **2g.**
Sodium **383mg.**

3 cups stemmed and chopped beet greens
2 lb. spinach, stemmed and chopped
½ cup chopped fresh parsley
2 cups unsalted turkey or chicken stock
¾ cup golden raisins
2 tbsp. unsalted butter
4 cups chopped onions
3 garlic cloves, finely chopped
2 tsp. chopped fresh thyme, or ½ tsp. dried thyme leaves
¼ tsp. salt
freshly ground black pepper
½ cup pine nuts, toasted
1 tbsp. fresh lemon juice
¼ cup brandy
2 cups dry bread crumbs

In a large pot, bring ½ cup of water to a boil. Add the beet greens and then the spinach and parsley. Cover the pot and steam just until all three are wilted — about four minutes. Drain and refresh with cold water. Squeeze out the excess moisture and set aside.

In a saucepan, bring the stock to a boil and reduce it to about ⅓ cup. Remove from the heat. Add the raisins and set aside to plump.

Meanwhile, melt the butter in a heavy-bottomed skillet. Add the onions and cook for about five minutes over medium-low heat, stirring frequently. Add the garlic, thyme, salt and pepper, and cook, stirring occasionally, until the onions are softened but not brown — about five minutes more. Add the raisins and stock.

In a large bowl, combine the greens, the onion mix-

ture, pine nuts, lemon juice and brandy. Mix in the bread crumbs. Allow the stuffing to cool before using.

EDITOR'S NOTE: *If you wish to cook the stuffing separately as a dressing, put it in a baking dish with an additional ⅓ cup of stock. Cover the dish with aluminum foil and bake the dressing in a preheated 325° F. oven for 45 minutes. Uncover the dish and return it to the oven for another 45 minutes. If you roast a turkey without stuffing, put the parsley stems, onion trimmings, a few garlic cloves, some thyme leaves and black pepper into the breast cavity for extra flavor.*

Red-Pepper, Corn and Eggplant Stuffing

Serves 10
Enough for a 10-to-12-pound turkey
Working time: about 30 minutes
Total time: about 30 minutes

Calories **217**
Protein **8g.**
Cholesterol **2mg.**
Total fat **4g.**
Saturated fat **1g.**
Sodium **258mg.**

1¼ cups unsalted turkey or chicken stock
3 tsp. virgin olive oil
¾ lb. mushrooms, quartered
¼ tsp. salt
2 medium-size eggplants, unpeeled, cut into ½-inch cubes (about 8 cups)
2 tsp. unsalted butter
1 large leek, trimmed and chopped, or 2 medium onions, chopped
2 tbsp. chopped shallots
2 red peppers, seeded, deribbed and cut into ½-by-1-inch strips
3 garlic cloves, finely chopped
1 tbsp. chopped fresh basil, or 1 tsp. dried basil
1 tsp. chopped fresh rosemary, or ¼ tsp. dried rosemary
1 tbsp. fresh lemon juice
1½ tbsp. red wine vinegar
2½ cups uncooked corn kernels, cut from about 5 ears of fresh corn
2½ cups dry bread crumbs

In a medium saucepan, bring the stock to a boil. Reduce the stock to about ½ cup and set it aside.

Heat 2 teaspoons of the olive oil in a large, heavy-bottomed skillet over medium heat. Add the mushrooms and sauté them for about one minute. Stir in the salt and eggplant, then cover. Cook until the eggplant begins to give off moisture — about four minutes. Uncover and cook, stirring frequently, for an additional 10 minutes. Transfer the mixture to a large bowl.

Place the skillet back on the burner. Heat the remaining 1 teaspoon of olive oil and the butter over medium heat, then add the leek or onions. Cover and cook for about one minute. Uncover and add the shallots, peppers, garlic, basil, rosemary, lemon juice and vinegar, and continue cooking until the peppers are tender — about two minutes more. Combine this mixture with the eggplant-and-mushroom mixture in the large bowl. Add the corn, bread crumbs and stock, and mix well. The stuffing should be thick but not sticky. If it is sticky, add more bread crumbs. Allow the stuffing to cool before using.

EDITOR'S NOTE: *If you wish to cook the stuffing separately as a dressing, put it in a baking dish with an additional ¼ cup of stock. Cover the dish with aluminum foil and bake the dressing in a preheated 325° F. oven for 45 minutes. Uncover the dish and return it to the oven for another 45 minutes. If you roast a turkey without stuffing, put the leek tops or onion trimmings, basil stems, a few garlic cloves and a piece of the lemon peel into the breast cavity for extra flavor.*

Turkey Galantine

THIS RECIPE FOR A GRAND AND ELEGANT PARTY DISH OFFERS A
BOLD DEPARTURE FROM THE CLASSIC GALANTINE.

Serves 10
Working time: about 2 hours
Total time: about 3 hours and 30 minutes

Calories **407**
Protein **55g.**
Cholesterol **165mg.**
Total fat **13g.**
Saturated fat **5g.**
Sodium **430mg.**

one 12 lb. fresh or thawed turkey
½ tsp. salt
freshly ground black pepper
1 tbsp. honey
Vegetable stuffing
10 to 12 large mushrooms, wiped clean
juice of 1 lemon
3 small leeks, about ¾ inch in diameter, trimmed to 8 inches in length and left whole, washed thoroughly to rid them of any sand
½ tsp. salt
2 small unpeeled yellow summer squash, cut lengthwise into 1-inch-wide strips about ¼ inch thick
2 small carrots, peeled, quartered lengthwise, with cores removed
2 tbsp. unsalted butter
1 onion, finely chopped
3 garlic cloves, finely chopped
1 lb. kale, stemmed and washed
1½ lb. spinach, stemmed and washed
¾ cup freshly grated Parmesan cheese
½ tsp. grated nutmeg
freshly ground black pepper
2 egg whites
Currant-and-wine sauce
2 large onions, cut into 1-inch pieces
2 carrots, cut into ½-inch pieces
1 celery stalk, cut into 1-inch pieces
3 garlic cloves, halved
1 tbsp. safflower oil
the turkey skeleton, neck, wings, heart and gizzard
1 bay leaf
2 tsp. fresh thyme, or ½ tsp. dried thyme leaves
¾ cup red wine
1½ cups chopped mushrooms, plus the mushroom trimmings from the vegetable stuffing
¼ tsp. salt
freshly ground black pepper
¼ cup currants

Place a thoroughly chilled turkey with its breast down, drumsticks facing you, on a wooden cutting board or other nonskid surface. Bend open a wing; using a boning knife or a small, strong, sharp knife, cut around the base of the wing and through the joint to remove the wing. Remove the second wing. Set both aside. Next, make a long slit from the neck to the tail, cutting through the skin to expose the long upper ridge of the backbone. Cut off the tail if it is still attached. With the knife blade held firmly against one side of the backbone, begin freeing the meat from that side of the bird. Using your other hand to lift away the skin and flesh, cut and scrape beneath the oyster-shaped morsel of meat shown at left and around and down the outside of the collarbone. Cut about one third of the way down the rib bones, working along the length of the carcass until you encounter the thigh joint.

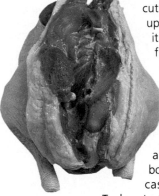

Cutting away the back around the collarbone, exposing the "oyster" and the thighbone.

To locate the thigh socket, grasp the end of the drumstick and pull the leg toward you. Cut away the meat and cartilage around the joint. Sever the joint by cutting around the ball where it joins the socket. Continue cutting downward to detach the leg; do not slice through the bottom layer of breast skin. Repeat these steps on the other side of the turkey.

Cut the skin and flesh from around the neck and collarbone so that the back meat comes away from the skeleton on both sides. Pressing the blade of the knife against the rib cage and then the breastbone, cut and scrape away the breast. Take care not to pierce the skin (that would allow filling to escape later) and stop when you reach the ridge of the breastbone. Cut away the breast on the other side, again holding the knife against the bone and halting when you reach the breastbone ridge. Scrape away the flesh on either side to expose the ridge and tip of the breastbone. Lift the skeleton with one hand. Then, starting at the tip of the breastbone, free the skeleton by cutting just beneath the entire breastbone ridge and through the cartilage with the knife, as shown at left. Be careful not to puncture the skin; there is no flesh between the skin and the bone at this point. Starting at the detached end of one of the thighbones, cut into the flesh on either side of the bone along its length. Scrape away the flesh from the sides and detached end of the bone. Holding the bone with

Cutting beneath the ridge of the breastbone to remove the skeleton.

one hand, scrape down its length to the joint to expose it, as shown at left. Sever the joint and tendons, and remove the thighbone. Repeat the process to remove the other thighbone. Now turn to the breast. Using your fingers to loosen and separate the connective membrane, peel the triangular fillets from the breast and set them aside (center left). Remove the white tendon from the thick end of each fillet by slicing through the flesh on either side of the tendon. So that the meat will uniformly encase the stuffing, make a horizontal cut in the thick part of each side of the breast as shown in the photograph below, at left. Unfold the resulting flaps into the triangular space at the top of the heart-shaped flesh. Carefully trim off excess fat and membrane. Replace the fillets on the breast. Cover the breast with plastic wrap and lightly pound the meat to flatten it evenly. Remove the plastic wrap and refrigerate the turkey until you are ready to stuff it.

Removing the thighbone.

Removing the white tendon from the fillets.

To begin preparing the stock for the sauce, preheat the oven to 400° F. Then put the onions, carrots, celery and garlic in a roasting pan, and toss them with the oil. Cut the skeleton and neck into pieces, and place these on top of the vegetables along with the wings, heart and gizzard. Put the pan in the oven. Roast until the bones are browned — about 30 minutes. While the turkey bones are browning, begin preparing the vegetable stuffing. Cut off the mushroom stems ¼ inch below the caps. Place the mushrooms on a cutting board, stems up, and slice off two opposite sides from each one so that the sides are flush with the stem; this allows the mushrooms to fit snugly against one another in a row when the stuffing is added. Reserve the trimmings for the sauce. Heat ¾ cup of water with the lemon juice in a nonreactive skillet over medium heat. Add the mushrooms, leeks and ¼ teaspoon of the salt. Cover and cook for seven minutes. Turn the leeks over and stir the mushrooms. Lay the squash strips on top, skin side up, and continue cooking until the leeks are tender — about five minutes. Drain the vegetables on paper towels and discard the liquid in the skillet.

Cutting a flap in the breast to flatten it out.

Add an inch of water to the skillet and bring it to a boil. Add the carrot strips, reduce the heat, and simmer until tender — about five minutes. Set the carrots aside with the other vegetables and discard the water. Melt the butter in the skillet over medium-low heat; cook the onion and garlic in the butter, stirring occasionally, until translucent — about 10 minutes.

Bring 6 quarts of water to a boil in a 10- to 12-quart pot. Add the kale and cook, covered, for five minutes. Add the spinach, stir, and cook for two minutes more. Drain the greens in a colander and run cold water over them until cool. Squeeze the greens firmly with your hands into two or three balls. Slice the balls into thin

sections. Put the sections in a large mixing bowl and combine them with the Parmesan cheese. Add the nutmeg, pepper, the remaining ¼ teaspoon of salt, and the sautéed onion and garlic. Whip the egg whites until foamy, and mix them into the spinach mixture.

Transfer the oven-browned bones and vegetables to a large pot. Deglaze the roasting pan with 2 cups of water. Add this liquid to the pot, and pour in enough water to cover the bones. Add the bay leaf and thyme. Bring the stock to a boil, reduce the heat to low, and simmer for one and one half hours, skimming foam from the surface as necessary.

To stuff the boned turkey, lay the bird on a work surface with its drumsticks pointing toward you; sprinkle the meat with ¼ teaspoon of the salt and some additional pepper. Spread the spinach mixture evenly over the breast to within one inch of the edges. Lay on alternating strips of squash, skin side down, and carrot. Position the leeks on top. Arrange the mushrooms stem side up in a tightly packed row down the center, as shown at left. Preheat the oven to 350° F. Thread a trussing needle with a long piece of butcher's twine. Wrap the thighs around the stuffing; if possible, have a helper hold up the sides of the turkey while you begin sewing it. (Any mushrooms that tumble out can be tucked back in later on.) Sew together the sides of the back to enclose the stuffing snugly. Stitch all the way to the neck, then sew up the wing holes. Use a short length of twine to tie the drumsticks together.

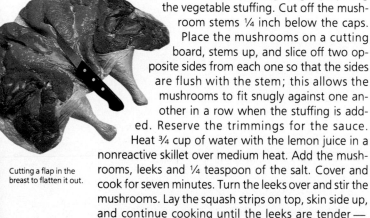

Arranging the vegetable stuffing on the breast.

Place the galantine on a rack in the roasting pan. Sprinkle the outside with the remaining ¼ teaspoon of salt and some more pepper. Use an extra-wide sheet of foil or two regular sheets crimped together to fashion a cooking tent about 18 inches longer than the pan. Lay the foil shiny side down over the turkey, and tuck the foil loosely around the inside edges of the pan. Place the pan in the oven and cook for 45 minutes.

Remove the pan from the oven and reduce the temperature to 325° F. Take off the tent and brush the outside of the turkey with the honey. Return the turkey to the oven for 45 minutes to an hour more; the galantine is done if the juices run clear when a thigh is pierced to the center with the tip of a sharp knife.

While the galantine finishes roasting, strain the stock into a 2-quart saucepan. Add the wine, chopped mushrooms and mushroom trimmings, salt, and pepper. Simmer until reduced to about 2 cups.

Remove the galantine from the oven and let it rest for 20 minutes while you finish the sauce: Add the currants to the stock-and-wine mixture and simmer for 10 minutes. Purée the sauce in a food processor or blender and pour it into a sauceboat.

Use a carving knife to cut the galantine into ¼-inch slices, supporting each slice with a spatula as you remove it. Pass the sauce separately.

3 *First steamed, then roasted, a duck stuffed with garlic, rosemary and pear is presented with watercress and stuffed tomatoes (recipe, page 117).*

Updating Some Old Favorites

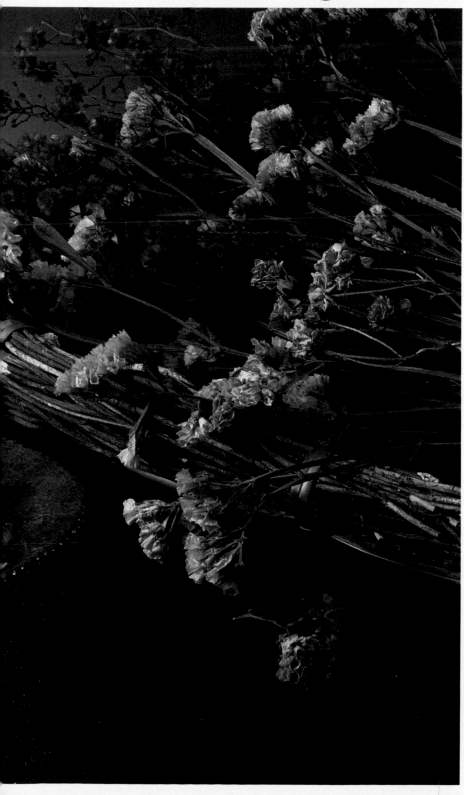

No poultry cookbook would be complete without duck, goose and squab. And two other birds demand inclusion: Pheasant and quail, once acquired only as hunters' bounty, are now being produced on game farms and brought fresh or frozen to market. They are well worth cooking, if not perhaps as family fare, then certainly as food for entertaining.

Of the five birds represented in this section, duck and goose are most readily available and receive the greater number of recipes. Fortunately, both can be cooked in ways that significantly reduce their fat content. Because most of their fat exists under the skin in a thick pad, it can be removed with the skin, or steamed or roasted away.

Roasting is the most popular method of cooking duck and goose. The trick is to prick the skin all over to permit the melting fat to trickle out during roasting. This should be repeated when the birds are about half-way done. At the same time, the fat that collects in the pan should be poured off or removed with a basting bulb, and discarded. The recipe for goose on page 121 first steams the bird to sweat out much of the fat, then roasts it. A goose so treated will emerge moist and tender from the oven under a sheath of crisply done skin, and the apple-and-red-cabbage stuffing will have none of the greasiness so often associated with goose.

Because of their tendency to put on fat, geese are generally killed when they are three to four months old and weigh between seven and 11 pounds. Their fat and bone structure make them appear meatier than they are. Thus it is a good idea to allow about three quarters of a pound of uncooked goose for a three-ounce serving.

Ducks are slaughtered young — at about seven or eight weeks of age and between three and a half and six pounds in weight. Like geese, they appear to have more flesh on them than in fact they do. Two types of duck are found in American markets, the so-called Long Island duckling and the Muscovy. The Long Island duckling is much more available and fattier than the Muscovy duck, which has a larger but stringier breast, making it a prime candidate for braising.

Ducks are usually sold whole, but can be cut up at home and broiled or sautéed. Lately, boneless duck breasts have become available in markets. Two recipes for breast appear in this section and call for the meat to be cooked lightly and served pink; any resistance to the idea will be overcome with the first taste.

Duck has much to recommend it nutritionally. A good source of protein, it is lower in cholesterol than turkey. And the meat itself is only slightly more fatty than the leanest sirloin, containing just 9.5 grams of fat per three-ounce serving.

Duck Breasts with Red Wine and Juniper Berries

Serves 6
Working time: about 45 minutes
Total time: about 45 minutes

Calories **474**
Protein **24g.**
Cholesterol **89mg.**
Total fat **11g.**
Saturated fat **4g.**
Sodium **187mg.**

6 duck breast halves, skinned and boned, with fat removed
1 tsp. safflower oil
¼ tsp. salt
Red wine and juniper sauce
4 cups full-bodied red wine
2 cups unsalted chicken stock
⅔ cup thinly sliced shallots, or 1 cup sliced onion
½ tsp. fennel seed
1 tbsp. juniper berries, crushed
8 black peppercorns
½ tsp. fresh thyme, or ¼ tsp. dried thyme leaves
1 bay leaf
2 tbsp. sugar
¼ cup balsamic vinegar, or 3 tbsp. red wine vinegar
1 tsp. honey
2 garlic cloves, crushed
½ tsp. cornstarch, mixed with 2 tsp. water

To begin the sauce, combine the wine, stock, shallots or onion, fennel seed, juniper berries, peppercorns, thyme and bay leaf in a nonreactive saucepan and cook at a slow boil until the liquid is reduced by half — about 25 minutes.

Meanwhile, melt the sugar in a small, heavy-bottomed saucepan over low heat, stirring constantly with a wooden spoon until the sugar turns golden brown. Standing well back to avoid being splattered, add the vinegar all at once. Stir to dissolve the sugar, then add this mixture to the reduced wine and stock mixture. Stir in the garlic and honey, and simmer the sauce for 10 minutes. Strain it, then return it to the pan. Cook the sauce, skimming occasionally, until it is reduced to about 1¼ cups. Stir in the cornstarch mixture and cook until the sauce is thick and shiny — about one minute.

Heat the oil in a large, heavy-bottomed skillet over medium-high heat and sauté the duck breasts for five minutes. Turn them over, sprinkle with the salt, and cook for three minutes more. Remove the breasts from the pan, set them aside and keep them warm. Deglaze the pan with about ¼ cup of water and ¼ cup of the sauce. Stir the deglazed pan juices into the sauce.

To serve, cut each breast diagonally into about 10 slices and arrange them on heated plates or a heated serving platter. Spoon the hot sauce over the duck and serve immediately.

SUGGESTED ACCOMPANIMENTS: *mashed potatoes; braised red cabbage or carrot and zucchini strips.*

Duck Breasts
with Sour Apple

Serves 4
Working time: about 20 minutes
Total time: about 30 minutes

Calories **308**
Protein **24g.**
Cholesterol **97mg.**
Total fat **18g.**
Saturated fat **7g.**
Sodium **152mg.**

4 duck breasts, skinned and boned, with fat removed
1 tbsp. virgin olive oil
⅛ tsp. salt
1 tbsp. unsalted butter
1 tart green apple, peeled, cored, thinly sliced and tossed with 2 tbsp. fresh lemon juice
1 shallot, finely chopped
½ tsp. fresh thyme, or ¼ tsp. dried thyme leaves
3 tbsp. balsamic vinegar, or 1 ½ tbsp. red wine vinegar
1 tbsp. honey
1 garlic clove, finely chopped
1 cup unsalted chicken stock

Heat the oil in a large, heavy-bottomed skillet over medium-high heat. Sauté the breasts on one side for five minutes. Turn them over, sprinkle with the salt and reduce the heat to medium. Continue cooking until the meat feels firm but springy to the touch — about three minutes. Remove the breasts from the skillet and keep them warm.

Add the butter to the skillet and sauté the apple slices for two minutes. Add the shallot, thyme, vinegar, honey and garlic, and cook, stirring frequently, until the apples are lightly browned — two to three minutes more. Add the stock and bring the sauce to a boil. Lower the heat and simmer the sauce until it is reduced by half — about 10 minutes.

Meanwhile, slice the breasts diagonally across the grain into ¼-inch-thick pieces. Fan the slices out on a serving platter or on individual plates. Spoon the hot sauce and apples over them, and serve immediately.

SUGGESTED ACCOMPANIMENT: *steamed broccoli florets.*

Duck with Mushrooms and Snow Peas

Serves 4
Working time: about 1 hour
Total time: about 3 hours

Calories **459**
Protein **30g.**
Cholesterol **69mg.**
Total fat **25g.**
Saturated fat **8g.**
Sodium **288mg.**

one 5 lb. duck, cut into four serving pieces
1 cup chopped onion
1 carrot, finely chopped
2 tbsp. flour
3 garlic cloves, finely chopped
¼ tsp. salt
freshly ground black pepper
3 cups unsalted chicken stock
1 cup dry white wine
3 or 4 fresh parsley sprigs
1 small bay leaf
½ tsp. fresh thyme, or ¼ tsp. dried thyme leaves
½ tsp. grated lemon zest
¼ lb. mushrooms, halved, or quartered if large
½ lb. snow peas, strings removed, blanched a few seconds in boiling water, refreshed in cold water and drained

Preheat the oven to 450° F.

Heat a heavy-bottomed skillet over medium heat and put in the duck pieces skin side down, without overlapping any of them. Sauté until the skin turns golden brown — two to three minutes. Turn the pieces and brown them on the other side — one to two minutes more. Transfer the duck pieces to a large, heavy-bottomed ovenproof casserole.

Place the casserole in the oven and bake it for 10 minutes; this renders the fat from the duck. Remove the casserole, spoon off the fat, and turn the pieces. Bake for another 10 minutes.

Remove the duck pieces from the casserole and pour off all but 1 tablespoon of fat. Add the onion and carrot to the casserole and stir well to scrape up any bits of meat that have baked onto the bottom. Cook the vegetables over medium heat for three minutes.

Return the duck pieces to the casserole and sprinkle them on one side with 1 tablespoon of the flour. Turn the pieces and sprinkle them on the second side with the remaining tablespoon of flour. Bake the casserole in the oven for an additional five minutes.

Reduce the oven temperature to 400° F. Stir the garlic into the meat and vegetables and sprinkle in the salt and pepper. Add the stock, wine, parsley, bay leaf, thyme and lemon zest, and bring the mixture to a simmer over medium-high heat. Place aluminum foil directly over the casserole contents, then cover with a lid and bake for 20 minutes.

Remove the duck pieces from the casserole. Pour the sauce into a small saucepan. Return the duck pieces to

117

the casserole and allow them to cool. Cover and refrigerate both the duck and the sauce until the sauce jells — two hours or overnight.

Spoon off the layer of congealed fat from the top of the sauce and discard it. Bring the sauce to a boil over medium-high heat, then cook it until it is reduced to about 2½ cups — 10 to 15 minutes. Pour the sauce over the duck in the casserole and reheat it over medium heat. Once the sauce is bubbling, add the mushrooms and cook for five minutes. Finally, stir in the snow peas, cover, and cook for one minute more. Serve very hot.

Roast Duck Stuffed with Pears and Garlic

Serves 4
Working time: about 30 minutes
Total time: about 2 hours and 15 minutes

Calories **407**
Protein **25g.**
Cholesterol **77mg.**
Total fat **27g.**
Saturated fat **10g.**
Sodium **212mg.**

one 5 lb. duck, rinsed and patted dry
1 tbsp. unsalted butter
15 to 20 garlic cloves, peeled, the large ones cut in half
1 lb. Seckel or Bosc pears, slightly underripe, cut into ¾-inch cubes and tossed with 1 tbsp. fresh lime juice
1 tbsp. fresh rosemary, or 1 tsp. dried rosemary
1 tsp. sugar
¼ tsp. salt
1 bunch watercress for garnish

Trim any excess skin and fat from around the neck of the duck. Remove any fat from the cavity. Cover the bottom of a large pot with 1 inch of water and set a metal rack or steamer in the pot. Bring the water to a boil on top of the stove. To help release fat while steaming, lightly prick the duck around the legs with a wooden pick or a skewer, taking care not to pierce the flesh below the layer of fat. Place the duck breast side down in the pot. Cover tightly and steam the duck for 30 minutes.

Preheat the oven to 350° F.

While the duck is steaming, melt the butter in a heavy-bottomed skillet over medium heat. Cook the garlic cloves in the butter, stirring frequently, until they begin to soften and brown — about 12 minutes. Stir in the pears, rosemary and sugar, and cook until the pears are soft — about eight minutes more. Set the stuffing aside.

When the duck has finished steaming, sprinkle it inside and out with the salt. Place the duck on a rack in a roasting pan, breast side down, and roast it for 15 minutes. Remove the duck and reduce the oven temperature to 325° F. Turn the duck breast side up on the rack. Prick the breast and legs of the duck. Fill the cavity with the pear-garlic mixture. Return the bird to the oven and roast it until the skin turns a deep golden brown — about one hour and 30 minutes. Cut the duck into quarters and garnish with the watercress.

SUGGESTED ACCOMPANIMENTS: *barley; broiled tomatoes.*

EDITOR'S NOTE: *The process of steaming followed by roasting helps to defat the duck considerably, resulting in a crisp skin and fewer calories.*

Roast Duck
with Cranberry Compote

Serves 6
Working time: about 45 minutes
Total time: about 2 hours and 30 minutes

Calories **596**
Protein **33g.**
Cholesterol **85mg.**
Total fat **30g.**
Saturated fat **10g.**
Sodium **389mg.**

two 4½ lb. ducks, rinsed and patted dry, necks chopped in 4 pieces and reserved
½ tsp. salt
2 onions, quartered
4 bay leaves, crumbled
Balsamic-vinegar sauce
4 cups unsalted chicken stock
1 onion, quartered
1 carrot, sliced into ¼-inch rounds
4 garlic cloves, crushed
½ tsp. dried thyme leaves
½ cup dry white wine
2 tomatoes, peeled, seeded and diced
2 tbsp. balsamic vinegar
⅛ tsp. salt
freshly ground black pepper
1 tbsp. grainy mustard
Cranberry compote
juice of 3 oranges (1¼ to 1½ cups)
1 cup raisins
12 oz. cranberries
1 tbsp. sugar

Trim any excess skin and fat from around the necks of the ducks. Remove any fat from the cavities. Pour enough water into a turkey roaster to fill it 1 inch deep, and set a metal rack or steamer in the water. Bring the water to a boil on the stove top. To release fat from the ducks without rendering their juices, lightly prick both legs with a wooden pick or a skewer, taking care not to pierce the flesh below the layer of fat. Place a duck breast side down in the pan. Cover and steam for 15 minutes. Remove the duck from the roaster; steam the other duck. Preheat the oven to 375° F.

Lightly prick the legs of both ducks again and pour off the juices from their cavities. Sprinkle the ducks inside and out with the ½ teaspoon of salt. Place half of the onions and bay leaves in the cavity of each duck. Put the ducks breast side down on a rack in a large roasting pan, and roast them for 30 minutes. Remove the ducks from the oven and reduce the temperature to 325° F. Turn the ducks breast side up and prick the entire skin. Return them to the oven and roast until the skin turns a deep golden brown — one hour and 15 minutes to one hour and 30 minutes.

While the ducks are roasting, begin preparing the sauce: Place the duck necks, stock, onion, carrot, garlic and thyme in a large saucepan. Bring the liquid to a simmer over medium heat and cook until it is reduced to 2 cups — about 45 minutes. Pour the enriched stock through a fine sieve and reserve it.

While the stock is simmering, make the cranberry compote. Put the orange juice and raisins in a saucepan and bring the liquid to a boil. Reduce the heat to low, cover, and cook for five minutes. Remove the pan from the heat and let it stand, still covered, for five minutes more. Purée the raisins and juice in a food processor or blender. Return the purée to the saucepan and add the cranberries and sugar. Bring the mixture to a boil, then reduce the heat to low, cover, and simmer until the cranberries have burst and almost all the liquid has been absorbed — about 15 minutes. Pour the compote into a serving bowl.

When the ducks are done, place them on a carving board while you finish making the sauce. Pour off the fat from the roasting pan and then deglaze the pan with the wine over medium-low heat. Add the enriched stock, the tomatoes and vinegar to the pan, and bring the liquid to a simmer. Stir in the salt, some pepper and the mustard. Raise the heat to medium high and cook rapidly until the sauce is reduced to about 1¾ cups. Carve the ducks and arrange the pieces on a serving platter. Pour the sauce over the pieces and serve the cranberry compote on the side.

SUGGESTED ACCOMPANIMENTS: *wild rice; steamed baby carrots.*
EDITOR'S NOTE: *The process of steaming followed by roasting helps to defat the duck considerably, resulting in a crisp skin and fewer calories.*

Goose Breasts with Blackberry Sauce

THIS RECIPE AND THE ONE THAT FOLLOWS USE ONE WHOLE GOOSE BETWEEN THEM. SINCE GOOSE BREAST IS NOT NORMALLY SOLD SEPARATELY, THE LEGS ARE RESERVED FOR A SECOND DISH THAT IS PREPARED THE NEXT DAY. RATHER THAN BEING CONSUMED IMMEDIATELY, THE DISH MAY THEN BE FROZEN FOR A LATER MEAL.

Serves 4
Working time: about 1 hour
Total time: about 1 day

Calories **333**
Protein **26g.**
Cholesterol **81mg.**
Total fat **14g.**
Saturated fat **4g.**
Sodium **217mg.**

one 9 to 10 lb. goose, gizzard, heart and neck reserved
2 cups red wine
¼ cup balsamic vinegar, or 3 tbsp. red wine vinegar
2 onions, cut in eighths
2 carrots, sliced in ¼-inch rounds
1½ tsp. fresh thyme, or ¾ tsp. dried thyme leaves
10 black peppercorns, crushed
1 bay leaf
2 tsp. safflower oil
¼ tsp. salt
freshly ground black pepper
Blackberry sauce
1 lb. fresh or frozen blackberries, several whole berries reserved for garnish, the rest puréed and strained through a fine sieve
1 tbsp. red wine vinegar
2 tsp. sugar
2 tbsp. gin

Lay the goose on its back. Cut through the skin where a thigh joins the body. Bend the leg outward to find the hip joint. Free the leg by cutting around the ball at the end of the thigh bone and through the socket. Repeat the process to remove the other leg. With a heavy knife or meat cleaver, chop the knobs off the drumsticks.

Slit the breast skin lengthwise along the breastbone. Keeping the knife blade pressed against the breastbone and then the rib cage, cut away each breast half. Pull the skin and fat away from the breast meat as much as possible with your hands, then use a small knife to finish the process. Pull the skin off the legs.

In a shallow dish, combine the wine, balsamic vinegar, one quarter each of the onions and carrots, one third of the thyme, and the peppercorns. Refrigerate the goose pieces in this mixture overnight.

Preheat the oven to 450° F.

To make the stock, first trim as much fat and skin from the goose carcass as possible. With a meat cleaver or a heavy knife, cut the carcass into two or three pieces. Trim and roughly cut up the giblets and neck. Place the bones and giblets in a heavy-bottomed roasting pan and brown them in the oven for 15 minutes. Then add the remaining onions and carrots and cook for 15 minutes more.

Transfer the contents of the roasting pan to a stockpot. Pour off the fat from the roasting pan, deglaze it with some water, and pour the liquid into the stockpot. Add enough water to the pot to cover the bones, then bring the liquid to a boil and skim off the scum. Reduce the heat to medium low. Add the remaining ▶

thyme and the bay leaf. Simmer the stock for two hours, then strain it into a saucepan and reduce it to about 2½ cups. Allow the stock to cool overnight in the refrigerator.

The next day, remove the breast halves from the marinade, reserving the legs and marinade in the refrigerator. Heat the oil in a heavy-bottomed skillet over medium-high heat. Sauté the breast halves for five minutes on their smooth sides. Turn them in the pan and sprinkle ⅛ teaspoon of the salt and some pepper over the cooked sides. Sauté the breast halves for three minutes more, then remove them from the skillet.

To prepare the sauce, skim the fat from the refrigerated stock. Add 1 cup of the stock to the skillet along with the puréed blackberries, 2 tablespoons of the marinade, the remaining ⅛ teaspoon of salt, the vinegar and sugar. Bring the mixture to a simmer over medium-low heat. Add the breast halves to the pan and simmer them for seven minutes, turning once. Remove them from the sauce and set aside to keep warm. Raise the heat to medium and pour in the gin. Cook the sauce, whisking frequently, until it is shiny and reduced to ¾ cup — about 15 minutes.

Cut the breast halves across the grain into very thin slices. Arrange them on a serving platter, pour the sauce over the top and garnish with the reserved whole blackberries.

SUGGESTED ACCOMPANIMENTS: *baby green beans; sautéed mushrooms.*

Braised Goose Legs with Shiitake Mushrooms

Serves 2
Working time: about 30 minutes
Total time: about 2 days

Calories **425**
Protein **28g.**
Cholesterol **97mg.**
Total fat **20g.**
Saturated fat **8g.**
Sodium **402mg.**

2 goose legs, skinned, refrigerated overnight in red wine marinade from the previous recipe
1 tsp. safflower oil
¼ tsp. salt
freshly ground black pepper
1 onion, chopped
1 carrot, sliced in ¼-inch rounds
1½ cups unsalted goose stock from the previous recipe
10 whole black peppercorns, crushed
3 or 4 fresh marjoram or parsley sprigs
4 garlic cloves, crushed
1 tbsp. unsalted butter
¼ lb. shiitake or button mushrooms, wiped with a damp paper towel and sliced

Heat the oil in a heavy-bottomed skillet over medium heat. Remove the goose legs from the marinade and reserve the marinade. Cook the legs on the first side until brown — about five minutes. Turn the legs and sprinkle them with ⅛ teaspoon of the salt and some pepper. Cook them on the second side until brown — about five minutes more. Transfer the legs to an ovenproof casserole.

Preheat the oven to 325° F.

Cook the onion and carrot in the skillet until soft — about five minutes — and add them to the casserole. Strain the marinade into the skillet through a sieve lined with a paper towel. Pour the stock into the skillet. Bring the liquid to a simmer and pour it over the goose legs. Add the remaining ⅛ teaspoon of salt, the peppercorns, marjoram or parsley, and garlic. Partially cover the casserole to allow some steam to escape. Braise the legs in the oven until they are tender — about one hour and 45 minutes. Remove the casserole and strain the sauce into a large, shallow bowl, gently pressing down on the vegetables to extract all their juices. Discard the vegetable solids. Set the legs aside in the casserole. Pour the sauce into a bowl set in a water bath. When the sauce has cooled to room temperature, remove the bowl from the water bath and place it in the freezer so that the fat will congeal quickly.

Heat the butter in a heavy-bottomed skillet over medium-high heat. Sauté the mushrooms until they are lightly browned all over — about 15 minutes.

Spoon off the fat from the surface of the chilled sauce. Pour the sauce over the legs in the casserole, add the mushrooms and warm over low heat until the sauce comes to a simmer. Serve immediately.

SUGGESTED ACCOMPANIMENT: *fettucini tossed with yogurt and poppy seeds.*

Goose with Apple-and-Red-Cabbage Stuffing

Serves 6
Working time: about 45 minutes
Total time: about 3 hours

Calories **445**
Protein **30g.**
Cholesterol **75mg.**
Total fat **17g.**
Saturated fat **5g.**
Sodium **322mg.**

one 10 lb. goose, with fat trimmed, gizzard, heart and neck reserved
½ lemon
1 tsp. salt
3 red onions, thinly sliced
2 cups dry white wine
2 lb. red cabbage, thinly sliced
2 tart green apples, peeled and cored, cut lengthwise into 8 slices
2 tbsp. grated fresh ginger
2 cups red wine
¼ cup red wine vinegar
¼ cup sugar
freshly ground black pepper
12 small shallots, peeled
1 tsp. cornstarch, mixed with 1 tbsp. water

Rinse the goose and pat it dry with paper towels. Prick the skin all over with a wooden pick or a skewer, taking care not to penetrate the meat lest the juices seep out.

Rub the goose inside and out with the lemon half, squeezing out its juice as you go. Rub the inside with ¼ teaspoon of the salt. Place half of the onion slices in the cavity of the goose. Tie the legs together with butcher's twine and tuck the wing tips underneath the back.

Pour 2 cups of water and the white wine into a large,

deep turkey roaster with a lid. Put a flat perforated steamer in the pan and place a large plate on it. Set the goose breast side down on the plate. Cover the pan, and steam the goose over high heat for 10 minutes. Reduce the heat to medium so that the liquid bubbles gently and steam still rises from its surface, and cook for 40 minutes more. Uncover the goose and prick its skin again. Steam for one and a half hours more.

Transfer the goose to a platter. Pour the cooking liquid into a bowl and set the bowl in a cold-water bath to reduce the temperature. Remove the bowl from the water bath and place it in the freezer so that the fat will congeal quickly.

While the goose is steaming, cover the giblets and neck with 4 cups of water in a saucepan. Add the remaining onion slices and simmer, uncovered, for about two hours. Strain the stock into a saucepan and reduce it over medium-high heat to about 1 cup. Discard the neck, giblets and onions. Refrigerate the reduced goose stock.

While the stock is simmering, make the stuffing: In a large saucepan combine the cabbage, apples, ginger, 1 cup of water, 1 cup of the red wine, the vinegar, sugar, ½ teaspoon of the salt and some pepper. Simmer the mixture for 30 minutes. Add the shallots and cook for 30 minutes more. Drain all the liquid from the stuffing and reserve it for the sauce.

Preheat the oven to 325° F.

Loosely fill the goose's cavity and neck with the drained stuffing. Close up the openings with metal skewers. Sprinkle the remaining ¼ teaspoon of salt over the outside of the bird. Place the goose breast side down on a rack set in a large roasting pan and roast it ▶

for 25 minutes. Turn the goose breast side up and roast it until well browned — about 35 minutes more.

Meanwhile, make the sauce. Take the cooled cooking liquid from the freezer. Remove the fat from the top and spoon the stock beneath it into a saucepan. Remove any fat from the refrigerated giblet stock and add the stock to the saucepan along with the drained stuffing liquid. Pour in the remaining cup of red wine and cook the sauce over medium-high heat until reduced by two thirds — approximately 35 minutes. There should be about 2 cups of liquid in the pan. Add the cornstarch-and-water mixture and whisk the sauce until it thickens.

Place the goose on a platter, spoon a little sauce around it and serve the rest in a gravy boat.

SUGGESTED ACCOMPANIMENT: *carrot-and-turnip purée spiced with nutmeg.*
EDITOR'S NOTE: *The process of steaming followed by roasting helps to defat the goose considerably, resulting in a crisp skin and fewer calories.*

Twice-Cooked Quail

ROASTING THE BIRDS AT HIGH HEAT GIVES THEM A CRISP, RICHLY COLORED EXTERIOR. THE BRAISING YIELDS A SAUCE THAT INCORPORATES EVERY BIT OF THE ROASTING JUICES.

Serves 4
Working time: about 20 minutes
Total time: about 40 minutes

Calories **397**
Protein **43g.**
Cholesterol **116mg.**
Total fat **22g.**
Saturated fat **6g.**
Sodium **402mg.**

8 quail (about 2 lb.)
freshly ground black pepper
½ tsp. salt
8 small sprigs fresh rosemary, or ½ tsp. dried rosemary
2 garlic cloves, thinly sliced
1½ tbsp. safflower oil
1 cup strong unsalted chicken stock (reduced, if necessary)
1 tbsp. Madeira

Preheat the oven to 450° F.

Season the cavity of each quail with equal amounts of the pepper, salt, rosemary and garlic. To truss the birds, place them on their backs and run a 9- or 10-inch piece of butcher's twine lengthwise beneath each one. Pull the ends of the string over the center of the breasts and knot them. Push the drumsticks under the string.

Spread ½ tablespoon of the oil over the bottom of a flameproof roasting pan that is large enough to hold the quail snugly. Brush the remaining tablespoon of oil over the quail and place them in the pan, breast side up. Roast for 20 minutes without basting.

Put the roasting pan on the stove top over medium heat. Combine the stock with the Madeira and pour it into the pan. Simmer the stock for two to three minutes, turning the birds over and over in the liquid as you work. Cut away the twine. Place two quail on each of four heated plates, and moisten the birds with one or two tablespoons of the sauce. Rotate each plate to distribute the sauce evenly around the quail. Serve the birds immediately.

SUGGESTED ACCOMPANIMENTS: *sautéed radishes; green beans.*

Quail Stuffed with Wild Mushrooms and Rice

Serves 4
Working time: about 45 minutes
Total time: about 1 hour

Calories **688**
Protein **50g.**
Cholesterol **116mg.**
Total fat **26g.**
Saturated fat **8g.**
Sodium **586mg.**

8 quail (about 2 lb.)
1 cup long-grain white rice
2½ cups unsalted chicken stock
¾ tsp. salt
2 tbsp. unsalted butter
1 cup dried mushrooms (about 1 oz.), soaked in 2 cups cold water for 20 minutes, then finely chopped, the soaking liquid reserved
1 celery stalk, finely chopped
1 onion, finely chopped
1 tbsp. fresh thyme, or ¾ tsp. dried thyme leaves
freshly ground black pepper
1¼ tsp. safflower oil
1 shallot, finely chopped
1 cup fresh pearl onions, blanched for 30 seconds in boiling water, drained and peeled, or 1 cup frozen pearl onions without sauce
½ cup Madeira
1 tbsp. cornstarch, mixed with 1 tbsp. water

Preheat the oven to 325° F. Combine the rice, two cups of the stock and ¼ teaspoon of the salt in an ovenproof saucepan over medium-high heat. Bring the liquid to a simmer, then cover the pan tightly and put it in the oven. Cook until all the liquid has been absorbed and the rice is tender — about 25 minutes — and let stand,

covered, for 10 minutes.

While the rice is cooking, melt 1 tablespoon of the butter in a heavy-bottomed skillet over low heat. Add the mushrooms, celery, onion and half of the thyme. Cook, stirring, until the celery is tender — about five minutes. Remove the skillet from the heat.

When the rice is ready, stir the vegetable mixture into it and set it aside uncovered. Raise the oven temperature to 425° F.

To prepare the quail, rinse out their cavities with cold water and pat them dry. Sprinkle the birds with ¼ teaspoon of the salt and some pepper. Stuff the quail with the rice mixture, reserving the excess stuffing for an accompaniment. Spread ¼ teaspoon of the oil over the bottom of an ovenproof casserole large enough to hold the birds in a single layer. Set the quail breast side up in the casserole and roast them until their breasts feel firm but springy to the touch — 15 to 17 minutes.

Meanwhile, start the sauce. Heat the remaining teaspoon of oil in a heavy-bottomed saucepan over low heat. Add the shallot and sauté it for two minutes. Stir

in the pearl onions, Madeira, ½ cup of the reserved mushroom-soaking liquid, the remaining ½ cup of stock, and the rest of the thyme. Cover tightly and simmer the mixture until the pearl onions are translucent — about 10 minutes.

When the quail are ready, transfer them to a warmed serving platter and pour the excess fat from the casserole. Put the reserved stuffing in a small baking dish, and cover it with foil. Turn off the oven and place the rice mixture in the oven to heat it through.

Place the casserole over low heat and deglaze it with some of the liquid from the saucepan. Return the mixture to the saucepan. Push the onions to one side, whisk in the cornstarch and water, and simmer for two minutes. Finish the sauce by adding the remaining ¼ teaspoon of salt, some pepper and the remaining tablespoon of butter to the saucepan. If the sauce is too thick, thin it with 2 tablespoons of the mushroom-soaking liquid. Pass the sauce separately.

SUGGESTED ACCOMPANIMENT: *steamed beet greens.*

just cover the bones. Bring the liquid to a boil over medium-high heat, skim off the impurities, and add the thyme. Reduce the heat to medium low and simmer the stock for 30 minutes. Add 2 more cups of water and simmer for one hour more. Strain the stock into a small saucepan and discard the solids. Reduce the stock over medium-high heat to 1½ cups.

Preheat the oven to 400° F.

Melt the butter in a saucepan over medium heat and cook the shallots in it until they are translucent — about three minutes. Whisk in the cream, and cook for one minute, whisking. Pour in ¼ cup of the stock and simmer for four minutes over medium-high heat, whisking constantly. Add the remaining stock and the cognac. Simmer for five to 10 minutes more, stirring occasionally, until the sauce has thickened slightly; there should be about ¾ cup of sauce. Stir in the remaining ⅛ teaspoon of salt and some pepper.

While the sauce is simmering, heat the oil in a large, heavy-bottomed ovenproof skillet over high heat. Sauté the squab breasts skin side down for three minutes on each side of the breast. Put the skillet in the oven and roast the breasts skin side up for six to eight minutes. Remove the breasts and let them stand for three minutes. With a small, sharp knife, cut each breast half off the bone in one piece. Then cut the breasts against the grain into thin slices. Arrange the slices on individual serving plates and spoon some sauce around them. Pass the rest of the sauce separately.

SUGGESTED ACCOMPANIMENTS: *green peas; acorn squash.*

Squab Breasts with Shallot-Cream Sauce

Serves 4
Working time: about 1 hour
Total time: about 2 hours and 30 minutes

Calories **391**
Protein **16g.**
Cholesterol **77mg.**
Total fat **25g.**
Saturated fat **10g.**
Sodium **156mg.**

four 12 to 14 oz. squabs, necks reserved, giblets discarded
¼ tsp. salt
1 cup dry white wine
2 onions, coarsely chopped
1 carrot, sliced in ¼-inch rounds
20 garlic cloves, crushed
10 black peppercorns, crushed
1 tsp. fresh thyme, or ½ tsp. dried thyme leaves
1 tbsp. unsalted butter
2 shallots, finely chopped
2 tbsp. heavy cream
2 tbsp. cognac
freshly ground black pepper
1 tsp. safflower oil

To remove the squab breasts, cut the skin between the legs and breasts and bend the legs down to the cutting surface. Remove each breast with its breastbone intact by cutting through the rib cage and around the wing socket. Sprinkle ⅛ teaspoon of the salt over the skin side of the breasts and put them in the refrigerator.

Cut up the backs, legs, wings and necks. Heat a large, heavy-bottomed casserole over medium heat. Sauté the chopped bones, watching that they do not burn, until they are well browned and the bottom of the pan is lightly caramelized — 10 to 15 minutes.

Deglaze the casserole with the wine. Add the onions, carrot, garlic, peppercorns, and enough water to

Pheasant Breasts in Parchment

Serves 4
Working time: about 30 minutes
Total time: about 30 minutes

Calories **271**
Protein **21g.**
Cholesterol **49mg.**
Total fat **7g.**
Saturated fat **1g.**
Sodium **172mg.**

4 pheasant breast halves, skinned and boned (about 1 lb.), the bones reserved for stock
1 tbsp. safflower oil
1 garlic clove, crushed
¼ tsp. salt
freshly ground black pepper
1 tbsp. finely chopped fresh ginger
1 shallot, finely chopped
½ cup pear-flavored liqueur
2 pears, quartered, cored, and cut lengthwise into ¼-inch-thick slices
½ cup unsalted chicken stock, or ½ cup pheasant stock made from the reserved bones
2 tsp. chopped fresh parsley

Heat the oil in a heavy skillet over medium-high heat. Rub the garlic clove over both sides of the breasts, then sauté the breasts for one minute. Turn them over and sprinkle them with the salt and some pepper. Sauté the breasts on the second side for one minute, then remove them from the skillet and set them aside.

Preheat the oven to 375° F.

Add the ginger and shallot to the skillet and cook them over low heat, stirring frequently, until the shallot is translucent — about two minutes. Remove the skillet from the heat and stir in the pear liqueur. Return the skillet to the stove and simmer, stirring often, until the liquid is reduced to about 3 tablespoons — two to four minutes more.

Add the pear slices and toss them gently to coat them with the pear liqueur. Pour in the stock and simmer until the liquid is reduced by half — about three minutes. Remove the pan from the heat.

Cut four sheets of parchment paper or aluminum foil, each about 12 inches square. Place a breast diagonally in the center of each square; spoon one fourth of the pears and sauce over each breast. Sprinkle ½ teaspoon of the parsley over each breast. Lift one corner of a parchment or foil square and fold it over to the opposite corner, forming a triangular papillote. Crimp closed the two open sides of the triangle, sealing the meat within. To crimp the parchment paper, make a series of overlapping folds along the open sides. Repeat the process to enclose the other breasts. Bake the papillotes on a baking sheet for eight to 10 minutes. Put the papillotes on individual plates and let each diner open his own to savor the aroma.

SUGGESTED ACCOMPANIMENTS: *lightly buttered noodles; arugula and radicchio salad.*

4 *A golden soufflé from the microwave oven stands ready to serve. The topping conceals a surprise filling of chicken stew and peas (recipe, opposite).*

Poultry in the Microwave Oven

A microwave oven presents a fast and easy way to cook poultry with a minimum of fuss. A whole, unstuffed three-pound chicken, for example, requires only about 20 minutes' roasting time, plus another seven minutes of standing time during which the meat continues to cook. Cut-up chicken parts need only six to seven minutes' cooking per pound — about one quarter the usual amount — and a five-pound turkey breast will be ready to take from the oven in just 40 minutes. Even a whole 12-pound turkey can be roasted to a fine succulence in a little over an hour.

In addition to its speed, microwave cookery offers some healthful bonuses. It can render more fat from chicken, say, than conventional methods do. And because the meat cooks for a much shorter time, fewer of its nutrients are lost.

Most microwave ovens are ineffective in browning foods since the air within the oven does not heat up the same way the food does and thus cannot affect the food's surface. Taking this drawback into account, Healthy Home Cooking has created eight microwave poultry dishes that please the eye as much as the palate by including colorful vegetables and appropriate sauces. Only one recipe calls for use of a browner, a glass-ceramic grill or dish with a tin-oxide coating that allows food to take on naturally a little of the appearance of meat roasted or baked in a regular oven.

The recipes have been tested in both 625-watt and 700-watt ovens. Though power settings often vary among different manufacturers' ovens, the recipes use "high" to indicate 100 percent power, "medium high" for 70 percent and "medium low" for 30 percent. To guard against overcooking a dish, use the shortest time specified; you can then test the food for doneness and cook it longer if need be. And remember that the food will go on cooking for several minutes after you have removed it from the oven.

Chicken Stew with Soufflé Topping

Serves 4
Working time: about 30 minutes
Total time: about 50 minutes

Calories **282**
Protein **26g.**
Cholesterol **53mg.**
Total fat **7g.**
Saturated fat **2g.**
Sodium **591mg.**

4 chicken thighs, skinned
1 butternut squash or 2 yams (about 1 lb.)
¾ cup evaporated milk
⅛ tsp. grated nutmeg
¾ tsp. salt
freshly ground black pepper
1 tsp. fresh thyme, or ½ tsp. dried thyme leaves
1 onion, finely chopped
1 celery stalk, finely chopped
2 tbsp. tomato paste
½ cup green peas
1 tsp. unsalted butter
6 egg whites

Prick the squash or yams in three or four spots and place them on a paper towel in the microwave oven. Cook on high for 10 to 12 minutes. Remove from the oven, cover with a paper towel, and allow to stand until tender when pierced with a fork — five to 10 minutes. Cut the squash or yams in half lengthwise, discarding the seeds of the squash, and scoop the pulp into a food processor or blender. Add the milk, nutmeg, ½ teaspoon of the salt and a little pepper; purée the mixture until smooth.

Rub the thighs with the thyme and some more pepper. In a 6-cup soufflé dish, combine the onion, celery, tomato paste, the remaining ¼ teaspoon of salt and a bit more pepper. Put the dish in the microwave oven and cook on high for two minutes. Stir the mixture, then add the chicken pieces, with their thicker ends facing the edges of the dish. Cook on high for four minutes. Turn each thigh to expose the other side, then mound the peas in the center. Rub the inside of the soufflé dish with the butter.

Transfer the purée to a large mixing bowl. If you are using a food processor, thoroughly wash and dry its work bowl. Whip the egg whites in the processor or ▶

with an electric mixer until they form stiff peaks. Stir about one quarter of the egg whites into the purée to lighten it, then fold in the remaining egg whites.

Add the mixture to the soufflé dish, filling it to the top. Microwave on medium low for 18 to 20 minutes, rotating the dish a quarter turn every five minutes; the top of the soufflé will crack slightly when it is done. Serve the soufflé immediately, while it is still puffy.

SUGGESTED ACCOMPANIMENTS: *watercress salad; French bread.*

Teriyaki Chicken

Serves 4
Working time: about 15 minutes
Total time: about 2 hours

Calories **168**
Protein **20g.**
Cholesterol **74mg.**
Total fat **9g.**
Saturated fat **2g.**
Sodium **121mg.**

4 large chicken thighs, skinned and boned
2 tbsp. low-sodium soy sauce
1 tbsp. dry sherry
½ tsp. honey
1 garlic clove, sliced
1 tbsp. finely chopped fresh ginger
⅛ tsp. crushed Sichuan peppercorns or crushed black peppercorns
1 scallion, the white part chopped and the green part sliced diagonally into 1-inch strips

To prepare the marinade, combine all the ingredients except the chicken and the green scallion slices in a deep bowl. Add the thighs and stir to coat them evenly. Marinate the thighs for two hours at room temperature or overnight in the refrigerator.

When you are ready to cook the chicken, preheat a microwave browning grill on high for the maximum time allowed in the grill's instruction manual. Remove the chicken from the marinade, wiping off and discarding the garlic, ginger and scallion. Set the thighs on the grill and microwave them on high for three minutes. Turn the pieces, sprinkle them with the green scallion slices, and cook on high for 90 seconds more. Serve immediately.

SUGGESTED ACCOMPANIMENTS: *steamed brown rice; cucumber salad.*
EDITOR'S NOTE: *If you do not have a microwave browning grill, cook the chicken in an uncovered baking dish for five to six minutes.*

Chicken in a Tortilla Pie

SALSA IS A VITAMIN-RICH SAUCE OF MEXICAN ORIGIN.

Serves 4
Working time: about 20 minutes
Total time: about 30 minutes

Calories **552**
Protein **54g.**
Cholesterol **170mg.**
Total fat **29g.**
Saturated fat **12g.**
Sodium **396mg.**

one 3 lb. chicken, wings removed, the rest skinned and quartered
½ cup unsalted chicken stock
¼ tsp. ground coriander
⅛ tsp. cayenne pepper
¼ tsp. ground cumin
1 green pepper, seeded, deribbed and finely chopped
4 scallions, finely chopped

| ¼ tsp. dried oregano |
| 1 tbsp. virgin olive oil |
| freshly ground black pepper |
| 6 oz. low-sodium cheddar or Swiss cheese, grated (about 1 ½ cups) |
| two 10-inch flour tortillas |
| ⅛ tsp. chili powder |

Salsa

| 2 large ripe tomatoes, peeled, seeded and finely chopped |
| 1 or 2 jalapeño peppers, seeded and very finely chopped (see caution, page 25) |
| 2 garlic cloves, finely chopped |
| juice of 1 lime |
| 1 tbsp. chopped fresh cilantro or parsley |
| ¼ tsp. salt |
| freshly ground black pepper |

Place the chicken pieces in a baking dish with the meatier part of each piece toward the edge of the dish. Pour in the stock, and sprinkle the chicken with the coriander, cayenne pepper and ⅛ teaspoon of the cumin. Cover the dish with wax paper and microwave on high for 10 minutes; halfway through the cooking time, turn the pieces over. Remove the breasts from the dish and microwave the leg quarters for two minutes more. Let the chicken stand in the liquid until it is cool enough to handle. Discard the liquid and shred the meat with your fingers.

Combine the green pepper, scallions, oregano, oil, black pepper and the remaining ⅛ teaspoon of cumin in a bowl. Cover the bowl tightly with plastic wrap. Cook for two minutes on high, then remove the bowl from the oven and mix in the shredded chicken.

In a separate mixing bowl, stir together the salsa ingredients. Add ½ cup of the salsa and half of the cheese to the chicken mixture. Place a tortilla on a large plate, cover it with the chicken mixture and put the other tortilla on top. Sprinkle the pie with the remaining cheese and the chili powder. Microwave on high until the cheese melts — about three minutes. Cut the pie into wedges and serve it with the remaining salsa.

Chicken Parmesan

Serves 4
Working time: about 15 minutes
Total time: about 40 minutes

Calories **368**
Protein **33g.**
Cholesterol **95mg.**
Total fat **17g.**
Saturated fat **5g.**
Sodium **695mg.**

8 chicken drumsticks, skinned, rinsed and patted dry
1 small onion, chopped
1 apple, peeled, cored and finely grated
1 tbsp. safflower oil
1½ cups tomato purée
2 tbsp. tomato paste
2 tbsp. Madeira
1 garlic clove, finely chopped
1 tbsp. chopped fresh basil, or 1 tsp. dried basil
¼ tsp. dried oregano
freshly ground black pepper
½ cup cornflake crumbs
½ cup freshly grated Parmesan cheese
½ cup plain low-fat yogurt

Combine the onion and apple with the oil in a bowl. Cover with a paper towel and microwave on high for one minute. Stir in the tomato purée, tomato paste, Madeira, garlic, basil, oregano and some pepper. Cover the bowl with a paper towel again and microwave on medium (50 percent power) for nine minutes, stirring the sauce three times during the cooking. Remove the bowl from the oven and let it stand.

While the sauce is cooking, prepare the drumsticks: Sprinkle them with some pepper. Mix the cornflake crumbs and the Parmesan cheese. Dip the drumsticks into the yogurt, then dredge them in the crumb-cheese mixture, coating them evenly. Arrange the drumsticks on a microwave roasting rack with the meatier parts toward the outside of the rack. Microwave on high for 15 minutes, rotating the dish once halfway through the cooking time. Remove the drumsticks and let them stand for seven minutes; then arrange them on a serving platter. Reheat the sauce on high for one minute and pour some of it over the chicken. Pass the remaining sauce separately.

SUGGESTED ACCOMPANIMENT: *spaghetti or ziti.*

Barbecued Chicken

PRECOOKING THE CHICKEN IN THE MICROWAVE ALLOWS FOR A
DRAMATIC REDUCTION IN GRILLING TIME.

Serves 4
Working time: about 20 minutes
Total time: about 40 minutes

Calories **345**
Protein **42g.**
Cholesterol **125mg.**
Total fat **11g.**
Saturated fat **3g.**
Sodium **390mg.**

one 3 lb. chicken, wings and backbone removed, the rest skinned and cut into serving pieces
1 small onion, chopped
1 garlic clove, finely chopped
¼ tsp. safflower oil
1 cup tomato purée
1 tbsp. cider vinegar
2 tbsp. chutney
4 drops hot red pepper sauce
2 tbsp. dark brown sugar
¼ tsp. dry mustard
freshly ground black pepper

Light the coals in a barbecue grill about 30 minutes before grilling time.

To prepare the barbecue sauce, combine the onion, garlic and oil in a bowl. Cover with plastic wrap and microwave on high for two minutes. Add the tomato purée, vinegar, chutney, red pepper sauce, brown sugar, mustard and pepper, and stir well. Cover the bowl with a paper towel and microwave on medium high (70 percent power) for three minutes. Stir the sauce again and microwave on medium high for three minutes more. Remove the sauce from the oven and let it stand while you precook the chicken.

Place the chicken pieces on a microwave roasting rack with their meatier portions toward the outside of the rack. Microwave the chicken on high for six minutes. Set aside any pieces that have turned from pink to white, then rearrange the remaining pieces with their uncooked portions toward the outside of the rack. Continue to microwave on high for periods of two minutes, removing the pieces that turn white.

Brush the chicken with the barbecue sauce. Grill the pieces over the hot coals for approximately 10 minutes, turning them once during the cooking and basting them often.

SUGGESTED ACCOMPANIMENT: *corn on the cob.*

Turkey Ring

Serves 6
Working time: about 20 minutes
Total time: about 35 minutes

Calories **266**
Protein **23g.**
Cholesterol **45mg.**
Total fat **12g.**
Saturated fat **3g.**
Sodium **314mg.**

1 lb. turkey breast meat, cut into 2-inch cubes
1 small onion, finely chopped
3 tbsp. plus 1 tsp. virgin olive oil
¾ cup dry bread crumbs
¾ cup low-fat milk
½ cup plain low-fat yogurt
¼ cup freshly grated Parmesan cheese
2 tbsp. chopped fresh basil, or 1 tsp. dried marjoram
freshly ground black pepper
1 zucchini, julienned
1 yellow summer squash, julienned
1 red pepper, julienned
2 garlic cloves, finely chopped
¼ tsp. salt

Combine the onion and 3 tablespoons of the oil in a small bowl. Cover tightly with plastic wrap and microwave on high until the onions are translucent — about three minutes. Uncover the onions and let them cool.

Grind the turkey in a food processor and mix in the bread crumbs, milk and yogurt. Add the onion, cheese, 1 tablespoon of the basil or ½ teaspoon of the marjoram, and some pepper. Operate the processor in short bursts to combine the ingredients.

With your hands, press the turkey mixture around the edges of a round dish 10 inches in diameter, forming a ring with a 4-inch-diameter hollow at the center. Cover tightly with plastic wrap and microwave on high for six minutes, turning the dish a quarter turn every two minutes. Let the turkey ring stand while you cook the vegetables.

Combine the zucchini, yellow squash and red pepper in a bowl with the remaining teaspoon of oil, the remaining tablespoon of basil or ½ teaspoon of marjoram, the garlic, salt and some pepper. Cover with plastic wrap and microwave on high for four minutes, stirring once halfway through the cooking time. Arrange some of the vegetables in a thin band around the outside of the turkey ring and mound the remaining vegetables in the center. Serve hot.

SUGGESTED ACCOMPANIMENTS: *corn muffins; red-leaf lettuce salad.*
EDITOR'S NOTE: *The turkey ring may be assembled in advance and then reheated for serving. To reheat the dish, cover it with plastic wrap or wax paper and microwave it on medium high (70 percent power) for four minutes, turning once.*

Cornish Hens with Barley Stuffing

Serves 4
Working time: about 25 minutes
Total time: about 1 hour

Calories **383**
Protein **29g.**
Cholesterol **94mg.**
Total fat **20g.**
Saturated fat **8g.**
Sodium **437mg.**

four 1 lb. Cornish hens, rinsed and patted dry
½ tsp. salt
½ cup barley
¼ cup freshly grated Parmesan cheese
2 tbsp. unsalted butter
1 small onion, chopped
½ cup finely chopped red pepper
2 garlic cloves, finely chopped
1 tsp. fresh thyme, or ¼ tsp. dried thyme leaves
3 oz. fresh mushrooms, wiped clean and thinly sliced (about 1 cup)
paprika

Add ¼ teaspoon of the salt to 1 cup of warm water in a small bowl. Microwave on high for two minutes. Add the barley and stir. Cook for nine minutes on high, stirring once after five minutes. Remove the bowl from the oven, cover it tightly with plastic wrap, and let it stand for 10 minutes. Take off the plastic wrap, add the cheese to the barley and stir.

Put 1 tablespoon of the butter in a bowl and microwave it on high for 30 seconds. Stir in the onion, red pepper, garlic and thyme. Cook for one minute on high. Add the mushrooms and the remaining ¼ teaspoon of salt, and mix well. Cook on high for two minutes, then combine this mixture with the barley.

Fill the body cavity of each hen with one quarter of the stuffing, taking care not to pack it tightly. Sew the cavities shut with a needle and heavy thread. Tuck the ▶

wing tips under the birds and tie each pair of legs together. Wrap each hen in plastic wrap and place the birds breast side down on a baking dish. Cook the hens on high for a total of 12 minutes, turning them over every four minutes.

Remove the birds from the oven and unwrap them. Melt the remaining tablespoon of butter in a small bowl by microwaving it on high for 30 seconds. Brush each bird with the melted butter and sprinkle each one liberally with paprika. Replace the hens on the dish, breast side up. Microwave them on high for a total of 12 minutes more, turning them every four minutes. Let the hens stand for about five minutes before serving.

SUGGESTED ACCOMPANIMENT: *Brussels sprouts.*

Roast Turkey with Tarragon-Cream Sauce

Serves 12
Working time: about 30 minutes
Total time: about 1 hour and 30 minutes

Calories **303**
Protein **45g.**
Cholesterol **89mg.**
Total fat **12g.**
Saturated fat **4g.**
Sodium **254mg.**

one 12 lb. turkey, rinsed and patted dry
½ tsp. salt
1 onion, chopped
2 tbsp. low-sodium soy sauce
1 tsp. paprika
1 tbsp. virgin olive oil
½ cup light cream
2 tsp. fresh tarragon, or ¼ cup chopped watercress
freshly ground black pepper
1 tbsp. cornstarch, mixed with 2 tbsp. water

Rub the cavity of the turkey with ¼ teaspoon of the salt and put the chopped onion inside. Tie the legs together and tuck the wing tips under the bird. Cover the wings and the ends of the drumsticks with foil.

Combine the soy sauce, paprika and oil in a small bowl. Brush the underside of the turkey with about half of this mixture. Put the turkey in a nylon-film oven cooking bag. Draw the bag closed, leaving an opening about the size of a quarter for steam to escape. Place the turkey breast side down in a large rectangular dish and microwave it on high for 15 minutes. Rotate the dish half a turn and cook the bird on high for 15 minutes more before removing it from the oven.

Pour the accumulated juices from the bag into a saucepan and set it aside; the juices will form the base for the sauce. Remove the foil from the wings and drumsticks. Turn the turkey breast side up and brush the wings and breast with the remaining soy sauce mixture. Close the bag loosely once more and micro-

wave the turkey on high for 15 minutes. Rotate the dish half a turn and cook on high for a final 15 minutes.

Remove the bird from the oven. Pour the additional roasting juices into the saucepan with the reserved juices. Let the turkey stand for 20 minutes, then test for doneness by piercing a thigh with the tip of a sharp knife; the juices should run clear. If they do not, microwave the bird on high for five to 10 minutes more.

During the standing time, prepare the sauce. Spoon as much fat as possible from the surface of the reserved roasting juices; there should be about 2 cups. Bring the liquid to a boil on the stove top and cook rapidly until it is reduced to 1½ cups — five to 10 minutes. Add the cream, the tarragon or watercress, the remaining ¼ teaspoon of salt and some pepper. Return the liquid to a boil. Whisk the cornstarch mixture into the sauce and cook until the sauce boils and thickens slightly — about one minute. Pour the sauce into a sauceboat; carve the turkey and serve.

SUGGESTED ACCOMPANIMENTS: *new potatoes; steamed artichoke hearts.*

EDITOR'S NOTE: *If you use a frozen turkey you may find that it will render more juice than a fresh one; either discard the excess juice or reserve it for another use. Although this recipe calls for a 12 pound turkey, you can easily cook a bird as large as 15 pounds in the microwave. Enclose the turkey in an oven cooking bag and microwave it on high for five minutes per pound, rotating the dish at three regular intervals during the cooking and turning the bird over halfway through the process. Avoid buying prebasted turkeys for microwaving: Their pockets of fat may explode during cooking. The pop-out thermometers imbedded in some turkeys will not be activated until the end of the standing time. Defrosting a turkey in the microwave is not recommended.*

Techniques

Cutting a Chicken into Serving Pieces

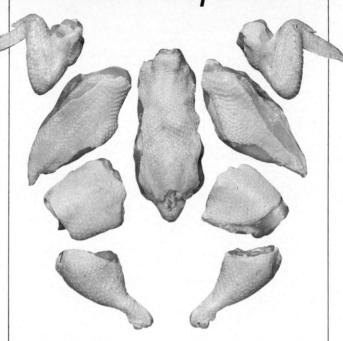

The waste-free and economical method of disjointing a whole chicken shown on these pages yields eight serving pieces (left). The backbone and any trimmings may be saved for the stockpot.

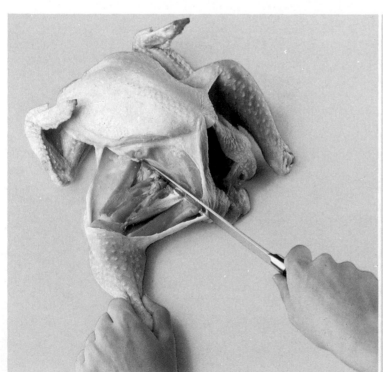

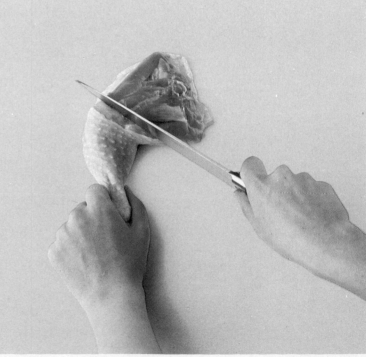

1 *SEVERING THE LEGS. Lay a whole chicken breast side up on a cutting surface. Pull one leg away from the body; with a chef's knife, slice through the skin between breast and thigh. Bend the leg until the thighbone pops out of the socket. Cut through the tissue joining the thigh to the body (above) to free the leg. Repeat the process to remove the other leg.*

2 *DIVIDING THE LEGS. Place a leg on the cutting surface, skin side down, and locate the hard, round ball of the joint that connects the drumstick and thigh. With a single firm stroke, cut down through the joint to sever the drumstick from the thigh (above). Repeat the process with the other leg.*

3 DETACHING THE WINGS. Pull one wing away from the body. With a sawing motion, work the edge of the knife blade into the joint (below). Sever the joint by slicing down through the cartilage and skin, separating the wing from the carcass. Repeat the process to cut away the other wing.

4 SPLITTING THE CARCASS. Holding the carcass steady with one hand, begin cutting from tail to neck through the thin tissue that joins the breast to the back below it. When you reach the rib cage, use a sawing motion (below) to sever the rib bones. Continue cutting to separate the breast from the back.

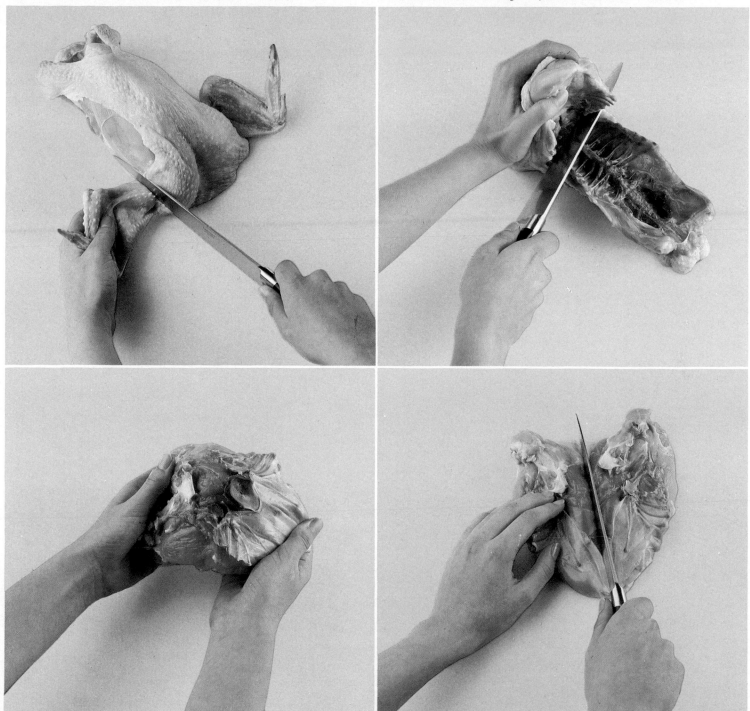

5 REMOVING THE BREASTBONE. Turn the breast skin side down and firmly grasp one end in each hand. Bend the two ends backward until the oval-shaped breastbone pops free (above). Pull out the breastbone with your fingers; this facilitates halving the breast.

6 DIVIDING THE BREAST. Lay the breast skin side down on the cutting surface. Using a firm, steady stroke to cut down the center line of the breast, split it in two. If you need to add strength to the cutting motion, press the palm of your free hand down upon the back of your other hand as you cut.

Boning a Breast Half

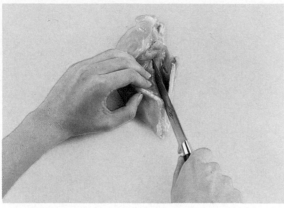

1 STARTING THE CUT. At the thicker edge of a skinned breast half, cut between the flesh and the bone with a sharp boning knife or utility knife, pressing the blade of the knife against the bone as a guide.

2 SEPARATING THE MEAT. With the tip of the knife blade, carefully cut the meat from the breastbone and ribs with repeated short slicing strokes, following the contours of the breastbone and rib cage. Detach the flesh in a single piece.

Boning a Thigh

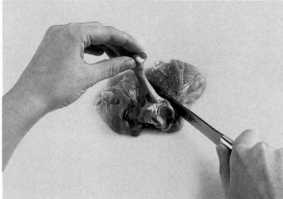

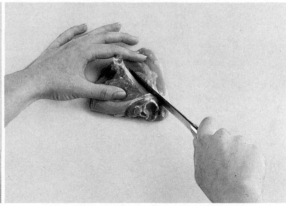

1 CUTTING TO THE BONE. Steady a skinned thigh with its smooth side down. Use a sharp boning knife or utility knife to cut as deep as the bone and along its length, pulling the flesh away from the bone as you work.

2 FREEING THE MEAT. With the tip of the knife, scrape and cut away the flesh clinging to the thighbone. Once most of the bone has been exposed, grasp one end of it and cut free the remaining flesh (above).

Trussing a Bird

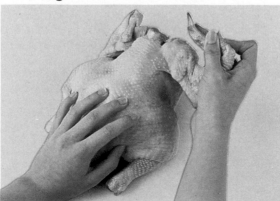

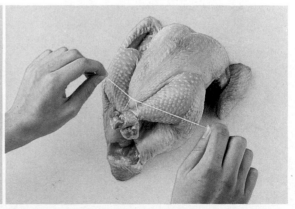

1 TUCKING THE WINGS UNDER. Place a whole bird breast side down on a work surface. Bend a wing tip up and back toward the neck until it lodges behind the shoulder. Repeat the step to secure the other wing.

2 TYING THE DRUMSTICKS. Turn the bird over and cross the drumstick ends over the tail, pressing the legs firmly against the breast. Loop a 2-foot length of butcher's twine several times around the ankles of the drumsticks to hold them together. Knot the twine and trim the excess.

Slicing Cutlets from a Whole Turkey Breast

1 *MAKING THE FIRST CUT. Lay a whole skinned turkey breast on a work surface with the ridge of its breastbone facing up. Then, using a sharp boning knife or utility knife, carefully cut down along one side of the breastbone ridge.*

2 *SEPARATING A BREAST HALF. Following the contour of the breastbone, carefully trim the meat in a single piece from the bone and ribs, using your free hand to pull away the flesh. Detach the long, thin fillet from the underside of the breast half; reserve it for another use. Repeat the process to detach the other half. Reserve the bones for stock.*

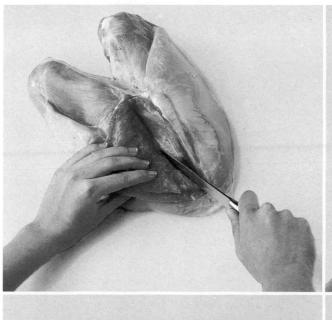

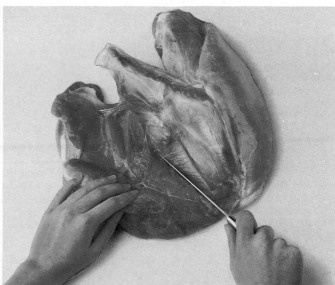

3 *SLICING CUTLETS. Starting at the tapered end of a breast half, slice diagonally across the grain of the meat with a slicing knife to detach the first cutlet. Cut successive pieces ¼ to ⅜ inch thick; slicing on the diagonal produces thin cutlets with maximum surface area.*

4 *FLATTENING A CUTLET. Lay a cutlet on the work surface and gently pound it with the flat of a large chef's knife, the blade facing away from you, until the meat flattens to about half its original thickness. Repeat with the other cutlets. The slices may also be flattened by placing them one at a time between two pieces of plastic wrap or wax paper, then pounding them with a wooden mallet or a flat-bottomed pan.*

Glossary

Aquavit: a colorless, dry Scandinavian spirit often flavored with caraway seeds.

Anise: the licorice-flavored seed of a plant native to the Middle East. It is used in certain curries and poultry dishes.

Balsamic vinegar: a mild, extremely fragrant wine-based vinegar made in northern Italy. The vinegar is aged for at least seven years in a series of casks made of various woods.

Basil: a leafy herb with a strong, spicy aroma when fresh, often used in Italian cooking. Covered with olive oil and refrigerated in a tightly sealed container, fresh basil leaves may be kept for up to six months.

Baste: to help brown and flavor a food, and keep it from drying out, by pouring pan drippings or other liquid over it during cooking.

Bay leaves: the pungent dried leaves of the bay or laurel tree, a Mediterranean evergreen, or the stronger-flavored leaves of its American cousin, the California bay tree.

Blanch: to partially cook food by briefly immersing it in boiling water. Blanching makes thin-skinned fruits and vegetables easier to peel; it can also mellow strong flavors.

Braise: to cook meat, vegetables or a combination of the two with some liquid over low heat. Braising can be done in the oven or on top of the stove. It helps to moisten and tenderize the food.

Buckwheat groats (also called kasha): the nutty-tasting seeds of the buckwheat plant, hulled, steamed, dried, and sometimes ground; often toasted to intensify flavor.

Bulgur: whole wheat kernels, or berries, steamed, dried and crushed. (Cracked wheat is raw crushed whole wheat kernels.)

Buttermilk: a tangy, low-fat, cultured milk product whose slight acidity makes it an ideal marinade base for poultry.

Calorie (or kilocalorie): a precise measure of the energy a food supplies when it is broken down for use in the body.

Caramelize: to heat sugar or a food naturally rich in sugar, such as garlic or onion, until it turns brown.

Cardamom: the bittersweet, aromatic dried seeds found in the pods of a plant in the ginger family. Often used in curries.

Cayenne pepper: a fiery powder ground from the seeds and pods of red peppers. Used in small amounts to heighten other flavors.

Cepes (also called porcini): wild mushrooms with a pungent, earthy flavor that survives drying or long cooking. Dried cepes should be soaked in water before they are used.

Chervil: a lacy, slightly anise-flavored herb often used as a companion to other herbs, such as tarragon and chives. Because long cooking may kill its flavor, chervil should be added at the last minute.

Chili peppers: hot or mild red, yellow or green members of the pepper family. Fresh or dried, most chili peppers contain volatile oils that can irritate the skin and eyes; they must be handled carefully *(see caution, page 25).*

Cholesterol: a waxy, fatlike substance made in the human body and found in foods of animal origin. Although a certain amount is necessary for body func-

tioning, an excess can accumulate in the arteries, contributing to coronary ailments. See Monounsaturated fats; Polyunsaturated fats; Saturated fats.

Cilantro (also called coriander or Chinese parsley): the pungent, peppery leaves of the coriander plant, often used in Mexican dishes.

Coriander: the earthy-tasting dried seeds of the coriander plant.

Couscous: a fine-grained semolina pasta, served with the classic North African stew of the same name.

Cumin: a slightly bitter spice used in curry and chili powders. Toasting gives it a nutty flavor.

Cutlet: in poultry cookery, a boneless, skinless slice of breast meat, cut diagonally across the grain.

Dark sesame oil (also called Oriental sesame oil): a dark, polyunsaturated oil with a relatively low burning point, most often used as a seasoning; it should not be confused or replaced with lighter sesame cooking oils.

Deglaze: to dissolve the brown particles left in a pan after roasting or sautéing by stirring in wine, stock, water or cream.

Degrease: to remove the accumulated fat from stock or cooking liquid by skimming it off with a spoon or blotting it up with paper towels. To eliminate the last traces of fat, draw an ice cube through the warm liquid; the fat will cling to the cube.

Fat: see Monounsaturated fats; Polyunsaturated fats; Saturated fats.

Fennel (also called Florence fennel or finochio): a vegetable with feathery leaves and a thick, bulbous stalk having a mild licorice flavor. It can be eaten raw or cooked. The leaves are used both as a garnish and as a flavoring.

Fennel seeds: the aromatic dried seeds from a variety of herb fennel, especially popular in Italian cooking.

Fillet (also called tenderloin): in poultry cookery, one of two long muscles found on either side of a bird's breastbone. The fillets are approximately one quarter the size of the breast muscle itself.

Fricassee: a variety of stew traditionally made from poultry and served in a white sauce.

Ginger: the spicy, buff-colored root of the ginger plant. Fresh ginger can be grated, chopped, julienned, or cut into thin rounds and crushed with the flat of a large knife.

Julienne: to slice into matchstick-size pieces, using a chef's knife, mandolin (manual food slicer) or food processor.

Juniper berries: the berries of the juniper tree, used as the key flavoring in gin. They lend a resinous tang to marinades and sauces for game and goose.

Kasha: see Buckwheat groats.

Mace: the ground aril, or covering, that encases the nutmeg seed.

Marjoram: sweet marjoram and its heartier relative pot marjoram are aromatic herbs related to oregano, but milder in flavor.

Millet: a nutritious whole grain whose nutty, mild taste makes it an ideal base for stuffings.

Monounsaturated fats: fats that do not raise the level of cholesterol in the blood; some types even lower the level. Olive and peanut oils are high in monounsaturated fats.

Nappa cabbage (also called Chinese cabbage): an elongated cabbage resembling romaine lettuce, with long broad ribs and crinkled, light green leaves.

Nonreactive pan: a cooking vessel whose surface does not chemically react with food. This includes stainless steel, enamel, glass, and some alloys. Untreated cast iron and aluminum may react with acids, producing discoloration or a peculiar taste.

Olive oil: any of various grades of oil extracted from olives. Extra virgin olive oil, which has a full, fruity flavor and the lowest acidity level, and virgin olive oil come from the first pressing of the olives. Pure olive oil is also extracted in the first pressing, but it has a lighter, less fruity taste as well as a higher acidity.

Paprika: a slightly sweet, spicy powder produced by grinding dried red peppers. The best type of paprika is Hungarian.

Pine nuts (also called pignoli): the seeds from the cones of the stone pine. The nuts' buttery flavor can be brought out by lightly toasting or sautéing them.

Poach: to cook gently in simmering liquid. The temperature of the poaching liquid should be approximately 200° F.; its surface should merely tremble.

Polyunsaturated fats: fats found in abundance in such vegetable oils as safflower, sunflower, corn and soybean. Polyunsaturated fats actually lower the level of cholesterol in the blood.

Prosciutto: an uncooked, dry-cured and slightly salty Italian ham, sliced paper thin.

Purée: to reduce food to a smooth, even, pulplike consistency by mashing it, passing it through a sieve, or processing it in a blender or food processor.

Recommended dietary allowance (RDA): the average daily amount of an essential nutrient as determined for groups of healthy people of various ages by the National Research Council.

Reduce: to boil down a liquid in order to concentrate its flavor or thicken its consistency.

Saffron: the dried, yellowish red stigmas (or threads) of the saffron crocus, which yield a powerful yellow color as well as a slightly bitter seasoning. Powdered saffron is less flavorful than the threads.

Safflower oil: a vegetable oil that contains the highest amount of polyunsaturated fats.

Saturated fats: fats found in abundance in animal products and coconut and palm oils; they raise the level of cholesterol in the blood. Because high blood-cholesterol levels may cause heart disease, saturated-fat consumption should be restricted to less than 10 percent of the calories provided by the daily diet.

Sauté: to cook a food quickly in a small amount of hot fat, usually in an uncovered skillet.

Scallopini: cutlets sliced or pounded thin.

Sear: to brown meat by exposing it briefly to very high heat, sealing in natural juices.

Sesame oil: see Dark sesame oil.

Sesame paste (also called tahini): a nutty-tasting paste made from ground sesame seeds that are usually roasted.

Shallot: a refined cousin of the onion, with a subtle flavor and papery, red-brown skin.

Shiitake mushroom: a variety of fresh or dried mushroom. The dried version should be stored in a cool, dry place; it may be reconstituted by 20 to 30 minutes' soaking in water before use.

Sichuan pepper (also called Chinese pepper, Japanese pepper or anise pepper): a dried shrub berry with a tart, aromatic flavor that is less piquant than black pepper.

Simmer: to cook a liquid or sauce just below its boiling point so that the liquid's surface barely ripples.

Snow peas: flat green pea pods eaten whole, with only stems and strings removed.

Sodium: an essential nutrient required for maintaining the proper balance of body fluids. In most diets, a major source of the element is table salt, made up of 40 percent sodium. Excess sodium may cause high blood pressure, a contributor to heart disease. One teaspoon of salt, with 2,132 milligrams of sodium, contains about two thirds of the "safe and adequate" daily sodium limit recommended by the National Research Council.

Soy sauce: a savory, salty brown liquid made from fermented soybeans and available in both light and dark versions. One tablespoon of regular soy sauce contains 1,030 milligrams of sodium; lower-sodium variations may contain half that amount.

Spatchcock: to split and flatten a bird, rendering it suitable for baking and quick grilling or broiling.

Squab: a young domesticated pigeon, usually sold frozen. Its weight ranges from 12 to 20 ounces.

Steam: to cover food and cook it in the steam created by a boiling liquid. It is an excellent means of releasing fat from a bird before roasting it. Steaming vegetables preserves the vitamins and flavors ordinarily lost in boiling.

Stir fry: to cook cubes or strips of meat or vegetables, or a combination of both, over high heat in a small amount of oil, stirring constantly to ensure even cooking in a short time. The traditional cooking vessel is a Chinese wok; a heavy-bottomed skillet may also be used.

Stock: a savory liquid prepared by simmering meat, bones, trimmings, aromatic vegetables, herbs and spices in water. Stock forms a flavor-rich base for sauces.

Tahini: see Sesame paste.

Tarragon: a strong herb with a sweet anise taste. In combination with other herbs it should be used sparingly, for its flavor may clash with rosemary, sage or thyme. Classically paired with chicken, it also marries well with turkey. Heat intensifies its flavor, so cooked dishes require smaller amounts.

Tenderloin: see Fillet.

Thyme: a versatile herb with a zesty, slightly fruity flavor and strong aroma. Of all herbs it is perhaps the perfect companion for poultry, intensifying the flavor of any bird.

Tomatillo: a small, green, tomato-like fruit used as a vegetable, covered with a loose, papery husk and having a tart flavor.

Total fat: an individual's daily intake of polyunsaturated, monounsaturated and saturated fats. Nutri-

tionists recommend that fats constitute no more than 30 percent of a diet.

Truss: to secure the wings and legs of a bird against its body. This can be done by tying or sewing them with cotton string or butcher's twine. The wings may also be tucked back under the bird. The compact shape thus achieved helps to avoid overcooking any part of the bird and keeps the skin from splitting at the joints; it also simplifies the turning process.

Turmeric: a spice used as a coloring agent and occasionally as a substitute for saffron. It has a musty odor and a slightly bitter flavor.

Virgin olive oil: see Olive oil.

White pepper: a powder ground from the same dried berry as that used to make black pepper, but with the berry's dark outer shell removed. Used as a less visible alternative to black pepper in light-colored foods.

Yogurt: a creamy, semisolid cultured milk product made with varying degrees of fat. Yogurt makes an excellent low-fat substitute for sour cream in cooking. To keep it from separating, add 1 teaspoon of cornstarch to ½ cup of yogurt before gently heating the mixture. Yogurt may also be combined with sour cream to produce a sauce or topping that is lower in fat and calories than sour cream alone.

Zest: the colored, outer layer of citrus fruit rind, cut or scraped free of the bitter pith. The zest contains the essential oils of the fruit.

Index

Picture Credits

All photographs in this book were taken by staff photographer Renée Comet unless otherwise indicated:

2 top and center: Carolyn Wall Rothery. 5 bottom: David DiMicco. 6: illustration by Joan Tartaglia for Perdue Farms Inc. 15 bottom: Taran Z Photography. 33: Steven Biver. 40: Michael Latil. 48: Michael Latil. 49: Karen Knauer. 57: John Burwell. 59: John Burwell. 75: Karen Knauer. 77: Steven Biver. 80: Michael Ward. 81 bottom: Taran Z Photography. 86: Michael Ward. 87: David DiMicco. 88: David DiMicco. 91: Michael Ward. 92: David DiMicco. 93: Karen Knauer. 94: David DiMicco. 95: Aldo Tutino. 96: David DiMicco. 98: Michael Latil. 100: Michael Geiger. 101-104: David DiMicco. 107-109: Michael Ward. 115: Michael Ward. 136-139: Taran Z Photography.

Props: Cover: tile, Design Tile, Inc., Tysons Corner, Va. 10-11: pitcher and sauce bowl, Marston Luce Antiques, Washington, D.C.; platter, Antiques by Ann Brinkley, Washington, D.C.; table, Kay Fries, Alexandria, Va. 13: Dansk Design, Falls Church, Va. 14: Kitchen Bazaar, Washington, D.C. 15: right, The Pineapple, Alexandria, Va. 16: The American Hand Plus, Washington, D.C. 20: Cambet de France, Washington, D.C. 22: Cambet de France. 25: Sandra Selesnick, Hollin Hills Potters, Torpedo Factory Art Center, Alexandria, Va. 27: Joyce Inderbitzin, Studio 24, Torpedo Factory Art Center. 30: Dansk Design. 32: Kitchen Bazaar. 35: copper pot, Williams-Sonoma, Washington, D.C. 38: platter, Liberty, Washington, D.C.; tiles, Ademas, Washington, D.C. 40: silverware, Martin's of Georgetown, Washington, D.C. 42: bowl, Moon, Blossoms and Snow, Washington, D.C.; tiles, Ademas. 43: The Kellogg Collection, Washington, D.C. 48: Marrakesh Restaurant, Washington, D.C. 52: Jeanne Comet. 53: Jane Beecham, Chevy Chase, Md. 54: Joyce Inderbitzin, Studio 24, Torpedo Factory Art Center. 60: spice rack, Placewares, Alexandria, Va. 63: Martin Block. 65: Paulette Comet. 67: The Sow's Ear, Alexandria, Va. 69: Liberty. 71: Nancy Brucks. 73: Portside, Alexandria, Va. 74: Frances Simmons Antiques, Alexandria, Va. 76: china, Clint Wolcott; table, Kathy Hardesty. 78: Portside. 79: Marc Westen Decorative Arts, Washington, D.C. 84-85: platter, The Market Square Shop, Alexandria, Va.; bowl, The Stabler-Leadbeater Apothecary Shop Museum, Alexandria, Va.; sauceboat, Worthington's, Vienna, Va.; table, Ruff & Ready Furnishings, Washington, D.C.; carving set, Gertrude Berman. 87: Uzzolo, Washington, D.C. 88: bowl, Valerie Gilman. 90: China Closet, Bethesda, Md. 91: Williams-Sonoma. 93: platter, Cavalier Antiques, Alexandria, Va.; forks, Marston Luce Antiques. 99: The American Hand Plus. 103: Appalachian Spring, Washington, D.C. 104: Lenore & Daughters, Alexandria, Va. 105: wicker, Spicer's Upholstery Shop, Alexandria, Va. 107: platter, The Two Harolds Antiques, Alexandria, Va.; tablecloth, Lenore & Daughters. 108: Moon, Blossoms and Snow. 109: left, The Two Harolds Antiques. 112-113: platter by C. Ned Foltz, Kate Bomberger, The Country Connection, Fabian House, Bowie, Md.; table, Frances Simmons Antiques; chair, Robert Godwin. 114: Martin's of Georgetown. 116: China Closet. 118: The Two Harolds Antiques. 119: Marjorie Ritter. 120: pot, La Cuisine, Alexandria, Va.; platter, Via Veneto, Washington, D.C.; tiles, Ademas. 121: China Closet. 122: plate, E. B. Adams, Washington, D.C.; bowl, Cambet de France. 123: plate, Arnie Aleskovsky; sauceboat, Iris Brucks. 124: plate, Jean Wilson; bowl, The Two Harolds Antiques. 128: China Closet. 129: Gossypia, Alexandria, Va. 132: The Two Harolds Antiques. 133: Robert Godwin. 135: Marjorie Ritter.

Acknowledgments

The index for this book was prepared by Dick Mudrow. The editors are particularly indebted to Ademas, Washington, D.C.; Nora Carey, Paris, France; China Closet, Bethesda, Md.; Chong Su Han, Grass Roots Restaurant, Alexandria, Va.; Kitchen Bazaar, Washington, D.C.; Brenda Tolliver, Washington, D.C.; CiCi Williamson, Arlington, Va.

The editors also wish to thank the following persons and institutions: The American Hand Plus, Washington, D.C.; American Heart Association, Dallas, Tex.; Jay Avram, Silver Spring, Md.; Leslie Bloom, Silver Spring, Md.; Ellen Brown, Washington, D.C.; Jackie Chalkley, Washington, D.C.; Nic Colling, Home Produce Company, Alexandria, Va.; Shirley Corriher, Atlanta, Ga.; Don Coubly, Art Center College of Design, Pasadena, Calif.; La Cuisine, Alexandria, Va.; Carolyn Dille, Rockville, Md.; Rex Downey, Oxon Hill, Md.; Marcia Fox, Alexandria, Va.; Richard Jeffery, New York, N.Y.; Lenore & Daughters, Alexandria, Va.; Martin's of Georgetown, Washington, D.C.; Suad McCoy, Vancouver, Canada; National Broiler Council, Washington, D.C.; National Cancer Institute, Bethesda, Md.; National Research Council, Washington, D.C.; National Turkey Federation, Reston, Va.; Lisa L. Ownby, Alexandria, Va.; Jane Peterson, Alexandria, Va.; Joyce Piotrowski, Vienna, Va.; Vivian Portner, Silver Spring, Md.; Ann Ready, Alexandria, Va.; Christine Schuyler, Washington, D.C.; Sharp Electronics Corporation, Mahwah, N.J.; Sandra Smith, Mount Lebanon, Pa.; Jimmy Sneed, Alexandria, Va.; Lyn Stallworth, Brooklyn, N.Y.; Kathleen Stang, Washington, D.C.; Straight from the Crate, Inc., Alexandria, Va.; U.S. Department of Agriculture, Washington, D.C.; Williams-Sonoma, Washington, D.C.; Jolene Worthington, Chicago, Ill.

The editors wish to thank the following for their donation of kitchen equipment: Le Creuset, distributed by Schiller & Asmus, Inc., Yemassee, S.C.; Cuisinarts, Inc., Greenwich, Conn.; KitchenAid, Inc., Troy, Ohio; Oster, Milwaukee, Wis.